I HAVE CHANGED

Jesse Owens
with
Paul Neimark

William Morrow & Company, Inc. New York 1972

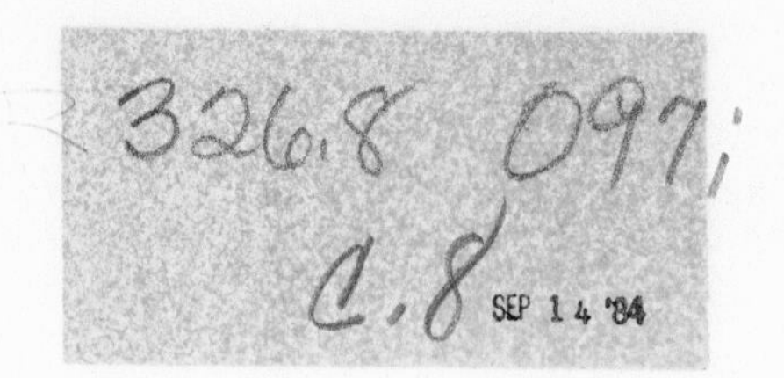

Printed in the United States of America.
Library of Congress Catalog Card Number 71-182956

To those who see
what it took me nearly sixty years to see—
That the choice
isn't between
changing or not changing,
but between changing for the better
or for the worse. . . .

PREFACE

Mr. James Landis
Senior Editor
William Morrow and Company
New York, New York

Dear Jim:

Enclosed is my second book. I don't think it's what you expected—it's not what *I* expected either.

Jesse

It was on a Saturday in the summer of 1970 when I began to realize I'd have to write another book.

I had just finished getting a haircut in a downtown Chicago barbershop. As always, everyone in the place—barbers and customers both—had given me a big hello when I'd walked in. I hadn't been at that shop for three months. Yet no matter where I go, Tallahassee or Timbuktu (and I've *been* to Timbuktu), almost everybody knows me. The few who don't, seem to think they should. I guess it's been that way ever since I won my four gold medals under Hitler's nose in the 1936 Olympics.

But that July morning I wondered if they knew part of me better than I knew myself. I thought I smelled more than shaving lotion and steam towels in that barber shop. I thought I caught the sour odor of a dark part of my soul.

I was using the washroom afterward. They must've thought I'd gone.

"What's that Jesse said to you about relocating?" another barber asked the one who'd cut my hair.

"Right," my barber answered. "Wants to move to Phoenix. Says the Chicago winters are getting him down."

Suddenly the black shoeshine man interrupted. "That's not why he's moving," the old voice rasped. "Jesse's moving 'cause colored moved into his neighborhood!"

Everybody broke up.

I didn't laugh. I winced. Not because it was true. It was a lie, maybe the worst lie anyone could mark me with.

But what went through me like a javelin was that *they* thought it was true.

They weren't bad guys. And they weren't fellows with any axes to grind against me. They were my *friends.* No, not close friends, yet possibly more important in my life than my close friends. Because this group of six or seven men were no different from hundreds of people I saw every week and had been seeing for thirty years. How many of the *rest* would say the same thing under the same circumstances?

I flushed the john, and walked out of the shop without saying a word. "I'll never go in *that* damn place again!" I said to myself as I left.

But wouldn't I? Wasn't *that* place *every* place?

Half a minute later, I was out on the busy sidewalk. People were passing by. Black, white, my generation, the generation of my three daughters, the coming generation. Just about every one of them looked at me with some kind of recognition. Some waved, some said, "Hi there, Jesse, how's it goin'?"

It wasn't going good. Something inside me was different.

I didn't know what for certain right then. All I knew was that I hurt—hurt worse, strangely, than after running my legs into cords of pain and my lungs into burning bags at the Berlin Olympiad, hurt more in a way than when my father and mother and most of my brothers and sisters had passed away, leaving me one of four instead of one of nine kids who started out in sharecropper's poverty within the suffocating prison of 1913 Alabama. Because all those deaths, agonizing though they were, had been inevitable, natural in a way.

What I felt inside me that July morning *wasn't* natural.

After my first book, *Blackthink*, went to the printer, regrets suddenly surged up inside me. In fact the minute Paul, my white collaborator, had put the galleys in the mail, a whole bunch of things that I wanted to change came to me.

There was that part where I said, "If the Negro doesn't succeed in today's America, it is because he has chosen to fail." Sure, I qualified it in the very next sentence. I'd said there were exceptions. But then I'd added that there were exceptions for the white man too. Down deep, I knew better. There aren't near as many exceptions if your skin is white. But I'd wanted so badly to tell the young blacks they *did* have a chance, if only they'd work twice as hard and turn the other cheek when the first one was maybe raw and open to the bone. I'd wanted to tell them *too* badly.

There was the chapter where I revealed the prejudice of black against black, about how a lot of Negroes with lighter complexions despised those with the darker skins. There was truth in it. I'd seen it a thousand times. But had I made too much of it? Wasn't the prejudice from people with white skins against brown or yellow or red much worse?

Most of all, there was my chapter on the militants. I'd divided them mainly into three categories—those who did it as a plaything, those who did it as a profit-thing and those who did it as an ego-thing. Sure, I left the door open—an inch—for the genuinely dedicated militant. But something else was even more disturbing: the story I told to fill in the blank.

It was about young Billy, the son of one of my closest friends, a good kid, a dedicated kid, who'd gotten acid thrown in his eyes and lost his sight and his will to live because he'd accidentally been in the right place at the wrong time. Billy—whom I'd known since he'd been a two-year-old toddler, who'd babysat for my grandchildren, who I'd proudly watched go through high school and the first year of college with straight A's, almost as if he were the son I'd never had.

Billy. A helpless, depressed, twenty-year-old boy, with no degree and no future, whose world had plummeted from political demonstrations and philosophy and history to trying to feel his way around his parents' apartment.

Billy—the *victim.*

Things usually don't stick in my craw very long, but, even in-between tens of thousands of plane miles and sometimes half a dozen speeches or interviews or raps a day for the next who-knows-how-many-days, my story of Billy stuck. Deep down, was that the way I *wanted* to see the "militant"? I'd had to admit there were good ones, but subconsciously was *I* throwing acid in all their eyes by warning the young, "If you become militant, baby, you're really taking your chances—look at Billy"?

The reviews of my book had all been good, every last one. But there was something almost suspicious about that, too. Isn't the guy who goes for records bound to foul now and then? "Jesse Owens thinks as straight as he ran"—"He understands much and tells it well"—"Sincerity and desire to help others be the human being he is have always been part of Jesse Owens"—"He deserves to be listened to *now*"—"Not a book filled with platitudes, but one man's serious thoughts on a serious problem," they went. The most glowing of all was from a fellow half my age, John Weigel in *The Chicago Tribune:* "The book deserves a wide readership," he said, "partly because Owens has kept in touch with every aspect of Negro life and tells the truth about it. More importantly, there is the essence of the man himself, a tough, compassionate, intelligent man who has a good deal to tell you about yourself."

And the praise didn't stop with reviews. More than one sociologist came out and declared that my analysis of the black militant was a genuine contribution. *Blackthink* won the Martha Cooper award for Best Human Relations book of the year. And, of course, friends by the hundreds were sending me copies to autograph. "Enemies" were silent. And why not? Had I ever really made any enemies, outside of Adolf Hitler? I was asked to write a syndicated newspaper column. A big paperback edition was scheduled to come out. Had I done it again? I'd even asked myself at first. Was it finally 1936 again after all those years?

Sure, I'd always been *known*—as I said, just about everybody recognized my name and most of them my face, too. But none of it compared to winning those four gold medals at Berlin or riding through the streets of New York afterward in a plush convertible with what seemed like half the people in the world lined up to cheer me. *That* was something to blow the mind of the eighth kid of a starving Alabama sharecropper, and it had blown mine. Down deep, no matter what the years had taught me, I guess I still wanted it all back again at the age of fifty-five.

Underneath it all, had *that* been the big reason why I'd written *Blackthink?*

I won't kid you, since that would be just another way of kidding myself. In the beginning I didn't sweat any of this very much. All the good things drowned out that nagging voice in the back of my head. Also, I was still "the world's fastest human," traveling over half a million miles a year, holding youth clinics and giving speeches all over America, flying to Africa for the Secretary of State to have the main street of that continent's newest nation named after me, coaching the American League baseball players how to run in the spring and trying somehow to get in a couple of rounds of golf a week in the fall (my one recreation) so I could keep my score within fifteen strokes of my age—a million, literally a *million* other things.

The pace didn't slacken, but the voice got louder anyway. The better the book went and the more 1970 became like 1936, the *more* disturbing it was. *Blackthink* was being received too damned well. I had said

I'd wanted to create a new, genuine third position in the United States, not just a sawed-off middle ground between "moderate" and "militant"—a fresh position that might unite the activists and the apathetics, the young and the old, black and white.

Well, *had* I really created a new position? Or was I just walking that same old tightrope—the tightrope of being worshiped for what I did in 1936, rather than being respected for what I'd done the 90 percent of my adult life since then? Had I reached out to new minds or was I only reaching the "minds" that were already committed?

And what about *my* mind? Could it be that even when I'd been what I figured (and what reviewers seemed to agree) was brutally honest about myself, that underneath, it was only because digging up a little Owens dirt wouldn't really tarnish the gold medals and would make the world admire me all the more?

I still haven't answered that question a hundred percent.

But I've answered some others. I know that moment in the barber shop was only the first of many. With each passing day, week, month, more things happened to make me want to re-examine myself, to change *Blackthink*, and not for any pats on the back it would get me. For what it could "get" me inside myself.

I want to tell you what those things were. Just as I want to tell you the parts of my face and my book that, even after everything, I wouldn't want to change a line of.

Paul put it to me another way not too long after *Blackthink* was published. "Even though you and I don't agree on everything, Jesse," he said, "I really loved working on that book. When we sent it off to be published, I felt we'd really accomplished something. But things have changed so damned much since we wrote it."

Yeah, baby. Things have changed *so* damned much since I wrote my first book.

Jesse Owens is one of those things.

WHAT CHANGED ME?

Adolf Hitler:

Some say you're still alive. I can't believe it because I can't believe anything so sick could survive a normal lifetime—let alone live with itself.

Even if somehow you are alive and hiding, my letter can only reach you, of course, through this book. And maybe what I'm trying to do is write a letter that should have been written thirty-six years ago. But then I was something more than mere years away from understanding that those who fight evil aren't necessarily good.

Jesse Owens

The lives of most men are patchwork quilts. Or at best one matching outfit with a closet and laundry bag full of incongruous accumulations.

My life—for a long, a very long time—was one of those rare, custom-made jobs. Remember Frank Merriwell, that famed fictional hero of a simpler world? He was so perfect they had to draw a lock of his hair out of place or else even the kids wouldn't have bought him.

Well, I didn't even have the lock of hair out of place.

For my whole life was wrapped up, summed up—and stopped up—by a single incident: my confrontation with the German dictator, Adolf Hitler, in the 1936 Olympics. The lines were drawn then as they had never been drawn before, or since. The Germans were hosting the Games and, with each passing day, were coming to represent everything that free people have always feared.

To me and my American buddies, most of the German athletes, the German officials, even the hundreds of thousands of German citizens who crammed the stadium those days in Berlin, weren't really our enemies. How could Lutz Long—the Nazi record-breaking broadjumper—be an enemy after he came over and put his arm around my shoulder and told me what I needed to do when I was on the verge of fouling out of that key event and maybe blowing the entire Olympiad?

But Hitler—he was something else. No one with a tinge of red, white and blue doubted for a second that he was Satan in disguise. Not that I was *too* involved with Hitler in the beginning. I'd spent my whole life watching my father and mother and older brothers and sisters trying to escape their own kind of Hitler, first in Alabama and then in Cleveland, and all I wanted now was my chance to run as fast and jump as far as I could so *I'd* never have to look back. Sure, when I glanced over at the German dictator's box and saw that constricted, twitchy face representing all that was bad in the world, it was nice to be on the other side. It was nice to be *leading* the other side, in fact. But I never doubted for a single minute that I *was* totally on "the other side," never dreamed there might be some parts of me—and of almost everyone—which resembled parts of *him*.

If I could just win those gold medals, I said to myself, the Hitlers of the world would have no more meaning for me. For *anyone*, maybe.

I won them—all four. And when I won the broad

jump, I really thought it all *had* come true. *He* wasn't even in his box glaring at the end. He couldn't take it, and had left. It was as if I'd destroyed Hitler and his Aryan-supremacy, anti-Negro, anti-Jew viciousness. The good guys had won. In fact, not just "the good guys," but the best possible "guy"—an American Negro. It was all very neat. Except for one thing. He returned to fight another day. Killed millions. Killed for many the ideals of the world. If I'd understood then what it was all about, if a lot of people had understood, it might have been different.

What I think I've learned, you see, is that—perverted as he was—Adolf Hitler wasn't really the villain. Even the millions of Germans who fought behind him—many of them who stood in Berlin stadium and applauded me—weren't the villains.

Ideas were the villains.

Ideas that allow a Hitler to come to power.

I'm almost sixty years old. The 1936 Olympic Games will always hold a golden glow for me, a glow that very few men know in their lives. But let's not make any fairy tale out of them anymore—or, rather, let's *make* the fairy tale of them that they and such things actually are. Because, as far as stopping the killing of six million Jews and the enslavement of sixteen million blacks in America, that Olympiad meant nothing. *Nothing.*

Remember the story of "The Emperor's New Clothes"—how all the adults would applaud approvingly at the splendor of the king's garments until one youngster finally cried, "But the Emperor's naked!"

In the last couple of years, I've wondered if the kids shouldn't read that story to the adults. Because we don't seem to understand it once we grow up. We cover ourselves thicker and thicker, year after year, hardly ever stopping, with imaginary protections against the pain of the truth. Finally, the agony of our self-imposed burden is far worse than confronting ourselves could ever be.

Whether it's my "legendary" Olympic experiences or the smallest details of my life, I'm going to try to turn that around. I'm going to try to be naked to you. To myself.

It's taking a big chance—my pen is actually unsteady this very moment as I write these words.

Because it will be cruelly cold out there if *you* can't be the same for me.

Eddie R. & Charlie Anonymous
St. Louis and Newark, U.S.A.

Dear Eddie R. and Charlie Anonymous:

You each wrote me letters, trying to hurt me—hurt me bad. You did—at first. But now, wherever you are, I want you both to know that you ended up helping me—a lot.

Jesse Owens

Like my race, it seems I've learned most from pain.

I happened to bump into our mailman one morning on my way out of the Chicago high-rise where Ruth and I lived before we moved to Arizona.

"Do you mind taking over, Jesse?" he asked. "I'm getting bent over carrying these books for you to autograph!"

I took the packages from him. There was the usual pile of letters too, as I remember. How could I forget after I found what was inside two of them? Invitations to speak, bills, maybe a check or two—I hoped. When I reached my car, I dropped the whole bunch on the seat because, as always, I was running late. If I recall that day correctly, I had a meeting in the Loop at 9:15, then had to get back down to my office on the South Side before grabbing a 12:30 plane to New York (due to return that same night at eleven). At the airport, I put the book packages in the locked trunk of my car, stuffed the mail in my inside coat pocket. When the plane was over Michigan, I began opening it.

It might seem strange to you, but until I wrote *Blackthink,* I'd never gotten a hate letter. I've been receiving anywhere from a dozen to three dozen pieces of mail a day (and a couple of special deliveries on Sunday) every day since I'd returned from the 1936 Olympics. If there'd been a morning when Ruth and I didn't get any mail, we'd have known the post office had gone out of business. And during all those years and all those letters, to say nothing of the countless phone calls and visitors dropping by out of nowhere—because I honestly felt I owed it to people to be listed in the phone book—I'd never really heard a hateful word. Even when I'd spoken on college campuses in the late sixties during the rise of black extremism, even when I'd confronted the most militant of the black militants and the wildest of the white leftists, I hadn't heard a hiss. Sure, I'd known criticism, and prejudice—the worst kind. *But not hate for me as an individual.* Somehow, my confrontation with Hitler had lifted me above that.

I expected it to change some with *Blackthink*. I expected the real extremists, far left *and* far right, white *and* black, the Establishment that I'd threatened *and* some of the anti-establishmenters I'd called cop-outs, to become real enemies. But they'd be the *correct* enemies. So if, after fifty-seven years of living, I was going to break out of neutrality and take a baton that was made of hot coals, if I was going to have cinders kicked in my face and even be gang-tackled as I ran toward the finish line—okay. But I wanted the race to mean something. If I was going to make some enemies, I wanted to make some new friends, too. In other words, if I was going to alienate 10 percent at either end of the spectrum—and I don't mean just the political spectrum, I mean the *human* spectrum—I hoped to create a new island for that uncommitted center who formerly hadn't known which way to turn.

And I'd gone the whole route, talked it in my speeches—which is mainly how I make my living—even followed the book with a syndicated newspaper series so as to reach an even wider audience with my idea of "the immoderate moderate."

That day over Michigan and Pennsylvania, I began to find out that I'd dropped the baton.

There was an invitation to speak at a Pennsylvania college. A request for me to hold a youth clinic in California. A thank-you for some work I'd done in Canada. A couple of bills. One check.

And two hate letters.

The first one read:

> Dear Jesse:
>
> That's a mighty fine story you're doing for all those papers. But why do you say you're black? Your real color is brown—for your nose. If it wasn't to start with, it sure would've been after what you've been putting it in to get on the good side of the murdering Black Panthers. Now *they are* black, boy—and I call you *boy* because you still should be a slave for some white man instead of running around loose like you do after us whites taught you to read and write. But the Panthers—they should be put in the ovens, just like the Jews were, every one of them. They don't give no breakfasts for kids—they kill and rape and rob. Not only their own trashy kind, but us whites. What they all really want for breakfast is our white women.
>
> Eddie R.
>
> P.S. You think if you don't brown-nose the Panthers,

they'll plug your black ass. But let me tell you, *boy*, that if you don't plug up your shiteating mouth, we'll put you back in leg irons like you belong.

The other letter was as different as it could be, and exactly the same:

Dear Jesse Owens:

Your series on the middle class black was very revealing. But it didn't reveal anything about us blacks—only about you and how you've become part of the fascist-capitalist conspiracy to systematically exterminate every black man in America. The only thing I wonder, Nigger, is why you don't see that when you've helped do away with all your own kind, that the white man will put a gun to *your* head, too. Or is it that you've been a Tom for so long that you figure by then the last little bit of color will have worn off your skin and you'll be white outside like you already are on the inside? Well, Nigger, you might get your wish sooner than you think. Somebody just might take a knife and scrape all the black away before it wears off from your playing up to Whitey.

Charlie Anonymous

As I said, I've known some rough times in my life, but, except for Hitler, I'd really never known hate against me personally until that afternoon flying to New York and reading—and re-reading—those two letters.

Sure, they were both from bigots. But they made a door spring open in my mind. Those two letters represented two irrational extremes. But did they represent more than that? Could they also have been a part of the thousands of books I'd autographed and hands I'd shaken? Had my words—my life—gone into the hands, the minds of that uncommitted segment I'd always wanted to reach?

I thought back on the year which had passed since *Blackthink*'s publication, tried to let those thoughts sink down into the depths of me. And for the first time, I realized I hadn't been a hundred percent honest with myself. For one thing, though I'd expected criticism, I'd also secretly expected my book to be a best seller. After all, I'd put *everything* into it—it was the story of my whole *life*. Yes, the book had done "well." But if it was *really* putting forth an important new idea about America's key crisis, shouldn't it have done even better?

When *Blackthink* didn't make the best-seller list—didn't get anywhere near it, in fact—I'd told myself that this wasn't the Olympics. This was a new arena for me. I couldn't expect a gold medal the first time out. And a lot of best sellers don't say anything, anyway. But underneath it all, something kept clawing away at me. Why hadn't the public *really* opened up to my book? More important, why hadn't the uncommitteds, no matter what their numbers were, let me hear from them? What did Malcolm X and Eldridge Cleaver have that I didn't have?

I know how open I was leaving myself by asking that question. I know it even sounds childish to say such a thing. But I felt it, felt it deep, and not in any kid's way. I wanted to *know* what *they* had that I *didn't.*

Because what I was seeing for the first time was that I hadn't created any third position, hadn't reached anybody who counted (or who hadn't been counted).

There was no third position.

There was no baton to carry. Unknowingly, I'd just poured two old recipes into a new pot and stirred like the world's fastest human, stirred so fast that sometimes it looked like they were actually mixing. But when the ingredients settled, it was all lumps. And now I had to take mine.

How could I have made such a mistake? I asked myself. It was one thing to almost foul out of the Olympics at twenty-three with the pressure of the whole world on my shoulders, or go broke forty months later because that same world had given me four gold medals but not one good job. It was another thing to have finally made it, to be fifty-seven years old, to put forth the product of my whole life and hear the world yell "Foul!"

Did it happen because deep down—no matter what I'd suffered (and I'd suffered a lot)—things were going right for *me* and my basic instinct was not to disturb them, not to upset the applecart? Or was it mainly that I believed, really believed, that what had come true for me *could* come true for everyone?

If I'm going to be brutally frank with you about my mistakes, I've got to be honest about the times I didn't make mistakes, too. Emerson said that if you believe that what you feel in your heart is true for all men, this is genius. In a way, *that* had been *my* genius. I had a kind of inborn ability to see the gold-medal lining in every cloud even with the storm of poverty or oppression all around. It had helped me not only to Olympic records but to a dubious "record" for having to bounce back from business failure after business failure. It was only natural to expect other people to do the same.

Natural—but wrong.

Not that anyone held it against me. That's why I'd never gotten a hate letter or a hate look even when I was telling ghetto grammar schoolers they could all get to college, even when I was imploring addicts to throw away their next fixes. As the plane circled New York's LaGuardia airport on that summer day in 1970, I saw that now was the time not to just attempt to inspire others with what was inside *my* head, but to truly try to get into *their* heads.

My mind riveted back to a Saturday at Ann Arbor, Michigan, three and a half decades before—to my greatest day in sports.

All the books say my "best" day were those days in Berlin. It isn't so. By far my finest one was May 25, 1935.

Earlier that week, it hadn't looked so fine. It looked like I wouldn't even be entered in the Big Ten meet that coming Saturday. I'd horsed around playing touch football and hurt my back. When I limped in to see Larry Snyder—a white man who was color-blind—I was bent over, grimacing in pain, and as ashamed of myself as I'd ever been. I had been working ten years for the one-in-a-million chance—where a black boy out of the rural South was concerned—to go to college and to compete in the Big Ten meet. And Coach Snyder had been working with me for countless hours since I'd been accepted at Ohio State University. He, my teammates, were counting on me. But, most of all, my two families: Ruth and Gloria—and my parents and brothers and sisters who'd let me stand on their shoulders with spiked cleats to get where I had.

"You can't run," Larry said to me. He never expressed much with his face, but the extra slump of his athlete's shoulders showed disappointment, and maybe a little anger, too.

I started to blurt something, but he answered me before it was out of my mouth. "I know—it's the biggest day of your life," he said, poker-faced, but holding up his right hand. "Yet you'd be risking all the *other* days, as far as track is concerned. *You can't run.*"

"I might be better by then, Coach," I implored. He stood up, looking down at me as his answer. I was an inch and a half taller than Coach Snyder. Bent over, I was a head shorter.

"Get a rubdown and some rest," he said. "Put wet heat on it. Chances are ninety-nine out of a hundred it won't help. But I'll keep your name in."

My hopes soared! There was a chance. A *chance*. I'd take care of myself like no one had ever taken care of himself. Somehow, some way, I'd be *ready*.

As I left Coach Snyder's office, I thought about when we'd moved up to Cleveland from Alabama. I'd entered grade school for the first time. The first two days I'd gone with Prentis or Quincy, but the third day all my brothers and sisters had to work—even though most of them were in grammar school, too—and I was sent off alone.

I got lost, wandering around for what seemed like hours, though it came to only forty minutes or so. I fought down the tears as each minute passed and was overjoyed when I saw the school suddenly loom up a block away after frantically turning my hundredth corner. As it worked out, the tardiness was lucky—I had to go see Coach Charles Riley—who just about ran the school, it turned out—to get a "late note." While writing it out, though, he asked me a lot of questions. He had a friendly, offhand way of talking that really made *you* talk. Finally, though, he said something. "I've seen the kids of southern sharecroppers before, but never one as thin as you."

I told him that I'd had pneumonia—though we called it a "powerful bad fever"—four times in the last three years.

"How did you pull through?" he asked.

"I guess somebody had to," I answered. "Three older kin didn't. By the time I was born, my mother knew more."

Charles Riley told me I would have to run if I wanted to *keep* surviving in the colder Cleveland climate. He brought me the food off his breakfast table four mornings out of five, though he never made me feel bad about taking it. I knew in my skinny bones that he was doing it because I was a kid—*not* a *colored* kid. Another reason was that the only time I could practice running was an hour and a half before school. In the night I had to clean house, after school I had a job delivering groceries and on weekends I worked in a greenhouse. So sometimes I ran when the sun had just come up, and that was the beginning of my becoming the world's fastest human.

As I limped out of Larry Snyder's office, I felt I *couldn't* let Mr. Riley down. He'd given me the legs, just as my mother and father had given me my very life by somehow pulling me through the pneumonias and getting me out of the South from which so many other Jesse Owens' had never escaped.

I took care of myself. Till I almost checked out from double pneumonia this last year, there wasn't a time in my life when I took better care. That Saturday morning came. I was standing straight, though in pain. I figured no one had to know about the pain, especially Larry.

He still didn't want to give me a chance.

"Larry—" I used his first name for the first time—"I've *got* to run today."

"Today could mean all the tomorrows," he said. "The Olympics next year."

"I've been waiting for *today* all my life," I pleaded.

Then I said something every sharecropper's son or ghetto militant has to feel. "When you come from where I did, you don't really believe in tomorrows."

That got him. "Okay," he finally answered. "But just the hundred." He meant the hundred-yard dash. "And the minute you feel anything different than right now, any twinge, any pain—pull up. Don't finish the race. Okay?"

It was easy to agree. I wouldn't be feeling any more pain than I was right then. Not that I was trying to play the hero. It was something else. I felt—really felt—as if my very survival depended upon being in the Big Ten competition. And winning. It sounds screwy to say it now, almost forty years later, but that's what I felt.

I jogged around a bit trying to warm up, but my back was bothering me too much to really work up a sweat. Finally, I walked over to where the other runners were—the best sprinters from the ten best schools in the Midwest, almost all of them white—and began digging holes in the dirt with my shoes. We didn't have starting blocks in 1935.

There was one sharp pain when I let my body down into the familiar crouch a few seconds later. But nothing could hurt me as much as being back sharecropping in the South again, and that's what not racing in the Big Ten amounted to in my brain. So when the starter told us to take our marks and then get set, I forgot everything except running. Like always, I watched his eyes out of the corner of my own.

There are only three things to being a champion sprinter. The first, of course, is having some natural speed. The second is being willing to stand the hurt so you can finish strong. Most people assume that because the distance is only a hundred yards the race is completely a matter of speed. The truth is that you begin getting tired about half way. Sure, you're not exhausted at the end as you are in the two-twenty- or four-hundred-forty-yard dashes. Yet you've still got to push when you don't feel like it those last thirty yards if you want to win.

There's one more thing to winning the dash, though. Getting off to a good start. As football player Jerry Kramer said in his book about the great Green Bay Packers of the sixties, he was able to help them beat Dallas in that unforgettable Super Bowl championship by getting off a split second before the ball was centered—but not so much that he was offside for the penalty. I'd always been able to get off a fraction of an instant before the other runners, not by listening for the gun as they did, but by watching the gunman's eyes. You can almost always tell from a man's eyes what he's going to do *next.* Too bad it takes most of us a lifetime to look into our own.

I started that split second before the gun exploded. Before the sound had died away, my feet were moving over the cinders as Charles Riley had taught me—like the ground was a burning fire I didn't want to touch, a full stride in front of all the other runners.

To a sprinter, the hundred-yard dash is over in *three* seconds, not nine or ten. The first "second" is when you come out of the blocks. The next is when you look up and take your first few strides to attain gain position. By that time, the race is actually about half over. The final "second"—the longest slice of time in the world for an athlete—is that last half of the race, when you really bear down and see what you're made of. It seems to take an eternity, yet is all over before you can think what's happening. Before I knew what was happening, I felt that sweeter-than-sweet tug of the finish tape against my chest.

I was so happy. I thought *that* was why there was no pain. Or maybe because right away Larry Snyder hurried over and told me I'd tied the world's record. But as a giant crowd formed around me and everyone asked questions, I realized the pain *had* gotten better. It wasn't gone, but it wasn't as bad anymore. Immediately, I broke away from the crowd and got Larry aside. "I can go in the broad jump, Coach," I implored him.

One event at a time that day, I persuaded Larry to let me compete not only in the hundred, broad jump and two-twenty, but the low hurdles, too. In the longer dash, I was able to pull away from Bobby Greaves in my last three strides, though it meant breaking the world's record. I had to set a new record to win the low hurdles, too. But in the finals of the broad jump, I was all by myself. I put a towel next to a place in the landing pit which was a little more than twenty-six feet from the takeoff board. Which was the *world's* record. Then I jumped so far past it they were actually cheering while I was still in the air.

When people hear the name Jesse Owens, they inevitably but unfortunately don't think of a flesh-and-blood human being, but of a superman. Even then, they think of the wrong "Superman"—the one who "vanquished" Hitler's superman, particularly in the broad jump. But the Olympic record I set was almost two inches less than what I did in the Big Ten meet. My record in Ann Arbor that day lasted twenty-four years, in fact.

I broke out that Saturday in Michigan, reached new limits. It wasn't only overcoming physical pain; it had to do with overcoming something psychological inside myself. Now, thirty-five years later as I sat in a plane circling LaGuardia Airport in New York, I wondered if I could break out again.

Twenty-four years is a nice, long time to have your record last. It's far too long to have some of your ideas last.

There are all kinds of sharecropping.

Eldridge Cleaver
Algiers, Algeria

Dear Eldridge Cleaver:

Ten years ago, if anyone would have told me I'd be writing a letter to a wanted criminal who'd fled the United States—and a black criminal—I'd have told him he was insane. Five years ago if someone had said I'd be writing a letter to the leader of the largest gang in history—and saying thank God he formed the gang—I would have laughed in his face. And maybe even day before yesterday if people had said that I'd be writing to an admitted rapist—and telling him that I thought he had less genuine crime in him than just about anyone I ever knew—I might have said, "Get the straitjacket and put me away."

But I'm going to say *all* those things right now. Maybe if I—and a lot of other people—had said them before now, this letter could have reached you in New York or Chicago or L.A. Maybe it wouldn't have had to be written at all.

Jesse Owens

To really understand me, you'll have to understand some *little* things about me.

In *Blackthink,* you see, I wrote only about the big things. Maybe that's why I only partly understood myself then. It's when you begin digging deep into *not* your big ideas and your memorable experiences, but the daily fabric which really is most of your life that you start seeing the forest which is way bigger than any few tall trees.

Not that I think every little thing about Jesse Owens is important. I'm afraid many of the big things don't mean too much, either. It's just that by looking past the confrontation with Hitler, I was able to learn what its *true* significance was. Through that, I found the lever in my own soul which let me change—in some of those small ways at least. One of the "little" things which helped me to locate that lever was finally understanding how I'd been living for thirty-five years.

The second week of March, 1971, was an example. In the space of less than seven days, I attended a track meet in Boston, flew from there to Bowling Green for the National Jay Cees, then to Rochester for the blind, Buffalo for another track meet, New York to shoot a film called "The Black Athlete," Miami for Ford Motor Company, back up to New York for forty-five minutes to deliver a speech, then into L.A. for another the same night.

What does it all mean? For one thing, it means half a million miles a year, year in, year out. *That* means still being the "world's fastest human," go-go-going at a pace I've honestly never seen anyone half my age take, getting on and off planes like most people get in and out of their cars, ticket in one of my hands and directions in the other, racing against my watch to make the flight, half the time not knowing exactly—actually *not*—where I'm going until the plane's in the air, being met at the other end by people who drive me to where I'm supposed to speak or work and then tell me where I'll be sleeping that night (*if* I'm sleeping over), finally being driven, usually at sixty miles an hour, to the next plane, hardly ever seeing it without the jets roaring. And in-between—except for the times I'm with youngsters, really alone with them—talking, talking, talking, always outgo instead of input, or at best machine-gun-fast back-and-forth, almost never time to *just* observe, listen, think, be alone. My hotel room isn't off-limits, either—there's always one more interview or autograph, one more decision or drink with somebody "important" before catching four, maybe five hours of sleep.

Don't knock it—it got me out of the ghetto.

Well, I'm going to knock it. I want to do whatever I can so someday there are no more ghettos. But some days I wonder if a lot of those poor kids aren't a lot richer than I am.

I know—easy for *me* to say. If I really mean it, why don't I trade places with them? I'll tell you why: Because I still believe I can have both—the good life *and* the deep one. And because I only feel what I feel *some* days.

One of those days was when I read Eldridge Cleaver's *Soul On Ice.*

It happened on a weekend in August of 1970. I finally had three days with Ruth and my family up at our new summer home in Michigan.

I'd "read" *Soul On Ice* before. Like I'd "read" a thousand other books.

I'd written about *Soul* in *Blackthink,* too—based on my "reading."

But when you're rushing from plane to plane and speech to speech—and writing some of the speeches on the plane in between writing your name on people's napkins or menus—you don't really read *any* book. You try. But there're never more than twenty minutes at any one stretch (and *that's* a rare happening) to actually sit and read or think about what you've read.

So most of the time I merely pick up a magazine, because I know I'm going to have to lay it down again in five minutes. On the rare days when I'm home with an entire afternoon empty in front of me, I run from where the books are, since that's where the phone and front door are too, run to the golf course where the world can't get at me.

So being famous did get me out of the ghetto, educate my kids, give my wife some of the things she deserved. But it also forced me not to skim just books, but often to skim life.

And it was starting to get me down. Even though I'd never said a word about it in *Blackthink,* I began to realize that it was one thing being "the world's fastest human," and it was another always being on the run. Little did I realize when I bought the summer home in Michigan two years ago (and buying it wasn't easy because, though I've almost always made a good living, I'm a soft touch and have never accumulated more than a couple of thousand dollars in the bank for any period of time) that it would finally give me the first real time in almost sixty years to be alone in depth with my family, and with myself.

It was our second weekend at the house when my eldest daughter put *Soul On Ice* in my hand again. She'd done it a couple of years before, but this time I read it, *really* read it. And it became one of the things which changed my life.

I'm not condoning Eldridge Cleaver's crimes of violence. But I do see as I never saw before how a kid from the ghetto could let himself be driven to these crimes. And as for his political "crimes," I'm not sure anymore who are the criminals and who are the liberators.

But I want to tell you what I am sure of.

I'm certain that what Eldridge Cleaver came from—being an animal—to what he was at his best and hopefully at least partly still is today—a poet, a philosopher, a lover in the deepest sense of the word—is possibly the greatest example in history of a man using his free will to change for the better. If this man could triumph over his poverty and his twistedness and his hate, without four Olympic gold medals and a worshiping world, couldn't I beat whatever ghetto was inside me?

Eldridge Cleaver had come up from one of the bitterest expressions of hate and twistedness—rape—to an understanding that "the price of hating other human beings is loving oneself less." What's more, he had seen how "self-hatred takes many forms; sometimes it can be detected by no one, not by the keenest observer, not by the self-hater himself. . . ."

As an athlete in the 1920's and 1930's, I learned something—not because anyone told me, but because you learned it or you lost. I learned that I was going to win. Learning that doesn't help much if you don't have ability and put in about five good hours a day for ten years. But there are also a lot of individuals *with* ability, and not just in the field of athletics, who work countless hours and never "win." Because they don't know they're going to win, which is the same as subconsciously knowing you're going to lose.

When I first achieved fame in the thirties, I found myself at a banquet with Babe Ruth one night. Some people had said the Babe didn't like blacks, but that was bull. Babe had been brought up a poor orphan, and he felt more of a kinship with anyone from any kind of ghetto than with all the fancy guys in the world who tried to ingratiate themselves with him. He had his faults, and they were king-size, but he always stayed true to his roots, even after he got to be the best-known, best-paid athlete in the world.

At that dinner, Babe and I found ourselves alone for a few minutes. "You gonna win at the Olympics, Jesse?" he asked straight out.

"Gonna try," I answered.

"Trying doesn't mean shit," the Babe said in his strangely raspy but high-pitched voice. "Everybody *tries. I succeed.* Wanna know why?" I nodded. Being with Babe Ruth twenty seconds was like knowing him twenty years. Both the bad and the good were right up there in front for you to see.

"I hit sixty home runs a few years back because I *know* I'm going to hit a home run just about every time I swing that frigging bat. I'm surprised when I *don't!* And that isn't all there is to it," he went on. "Because *I* know it, the pitchers, *they* know it too." He whispered it mischievously. "They're pretty sure I'm going to hit a homer every time." Then he broke into a boisterous laugh.

There's a connection between the inner confidence that lets you win races with your legs and the confidence that helps you to win those hundreds of inner races inside yourself each day of your life, the "confidence" that *won't* let you hate yourself. Eldridge Cleaver made me wonder if sometimes, though winning for the world, I wasn't running a hateful race away from part of myself. Especially when he quoted Norman Mailer, "Being a man is the continuing battle of one's life, and one loses a bit of manhood with every stale compromise to the authority of any power in which one does not believe." Or when he wrote those mind-blowing love letters to Beverly Axelrod, his white lawyer. I've never read such love letters. A man who could love *that* much, that *deep*, deserved more than a hearing.

I finished *Soul On Ice* shortly after lunch. At about one thirty, our kids started arriving for a family weekend. Gloria and her husband Hemp (Malcolm Hemphill), their two girls, Beverly Prather and her husband Donald, their girls, Marlene Rankin and her Stuart—and my first grandson.

We swam, we ate, we talked. We disagreed on small things—like any family. My three girls love and respect their parents, thank God, but that doesn't mean they'd gone our way. Mostly, they'd gone Eldridge's way.

Even with what Eldridge Cleaver gave me that morning, he'll never mean to me what he does to most of them. Because, though it might sound rigid and square and establishment and even *prejudiced,* I can never completely get over the fact that he raped a woman. But what I also saw was: If that's where he started, if *he'd* begun in the most abject sureness of *never winning,* then he'd come a helluva lot farther than *I* had. The extreme of love he went to from the extreme of hate where he'd been born spans the whole universe of the human spirit.

I looked at the faces of each member of my family that day. And I wondered if I had shown them all the love I had in *my* heart for *them.* Or had I let our petty disagreements and my busyness get the best of our relationships? Did I want to play the unflawed father-figure forever?

I've always said how Martin Luther King was one of my very few heroes. It was because, despite all *his* faults, he was perfect. Yes, in a way—*perfect.*

Because he had no hate.

Martin's benevolence toward the world was a kind

of prophetic, all-encompassing feeling which knew no hint of bitterness or pettiness. Even in those personal moments when I was alone with him and he would show a rare anger toward bigotry and oppression and the white man, even when he admitted to me once that he felt "hate—but only for a moment, Jesse," I knew that Martin wasn't really even feeling hate.

In a way, Martin Luther King, Jr., actually didn't know what hate was.

Eldridge Cleaver knows too well. Yet he has also already left all of us an infinite legacy of love.

To ignore it, a human soul would have to be packed in ice a mile thick.

Moe and Dorothy
San Francisco, California

Dear Moe and Dorothy:

Where in the hell are you now?

Jesse Owens

I said that Martin Luther King, Jr., didn't have a single drop of ice water in his soul. That isn't true of most of his followers, I'm afraid. Sadly, Martin's death has taught me even more than did his life.

I got the first hint of that when two white friends—I *thought* they were friends—called me long distance the day after the "revelations" about Martin's alleged sexual promiscuity were made public. Moe and Dorothy are a couple I met a few years ago when I was on the west coast setting up some ghetto recreation centers. The strongest bond we had in common was our feeling for the work Martin was doing—for Martin himself, really. When he'd been shot, they were emotionally wiped out, just as I was.

But they didn't sound wiped out when they called, from their four-hundred-dollar-a-month apartment, he on the sunroom phone, she on the extension.

"Jesse," Moe said first, after the usual *how-are-you's*, "tell you why I called. Did you read this stuff about Martin?"

Without any expression in my voice, I said I had. I could smell it coming somehow.

"Well," he went on, "we don't know how to make sense of it. And because we knew him—although we certainly didn't know *that*—everyone in our circle is asking us about it."

I didn't say anything. Their *circle*.

"Well, Jesse," Dorothy broke in, "you called Martin absolutely good in your own book. Is it still humanly possible now for you to feel that?"

"Why shouldn't I?"

From there on, the conversation tumbled like a steeplechase runner with cement boots. There was no way to show these people that Martin could have made the mistakes the paper said he had and still be absolutely good in the sense that I meant it, in the most important sense.

The next morning I flew to Boston. When I arrived back in Chicago the following day, one of my oldest buddies, "Blue," met me at the airport. "Hey, Jesse," he greeted, "did you hear that jazz about old Martin?"

"You mean what J. Edgar Hoover was supposed to have taped?"

He winked as he slapped me on the arm. "You never told me Martin did a lot more than preaching!"

I lost my temper. Moe and Dorothy—and the dozen others in between—were understandable, even if they were irritating as hell. But not Blue.

"I didn't know it for sure," I said. "I still don't know for sure. I don't know anything about anyone unless I'm there in the bedroom watching them beat their wife or make love to somebody else's."

"Sure, sure," he said in a low, too damn confidential tone. "So you didn't *know* it, you old black intellectual, you. But how come we've talked about him all these years and you never said what you *nearly* knew?"

"Because *you* wouldn't have known how to take it, baby," I seethed.

"Listen to *him* talk!" Blue bellowed. "You're no saint, either, Jesse! Though I don't *know* that, of course. . . ."

I "know" I'm no saint. Who is? A man doesn't live in this world sixty years without making mistakes. And I've had the opportunity to make some worse ones than most people. I'm not excusing them. But I will tell you something: Even though a man tries to change, tries to grow, to be better, what gives him the very will to do it is the something inside himself that'll hopefully never change. I've done stupid things, and possibly they turned out to be cruel things. I'll regret them till the day I die. But to be brutally honest, there's a part of me that is still pure, a part I've never sold out.

Martin's pure part was like an ocean to my stream. But where are the Moes and Dorothys now? Oh, they honor his memory. But they desecrate his meaning. When the "news" about his "sordid" side came out, whites and blacks alike began pawing like vultures at those newly discovered clay feet. Sure, a lot of people said, "So what?" But too many of those were the cynics who never believed in anything anyway. And what hit me hardest of all wasn't even that first punch in the gut from the Moes and Dorothys and Blues, it was the kick in the groin from a country that seemed to accept (even if it didn't like) a government that intruded upon the privacy of a man's bedroom.

The "justification" was that Martin had "Communist-influenced" people around him. What I saw—and it brought me closer to bitterly hating the white man, *every* white man, than I'd been in a long, long time—was a seventy-five-year-old, never-married whitey doing what amounts to looking through the keyhole of a thirty-five-year-old married black man with four kids. And, by the way, Martin wasn't a Communist any more than I am. Though it *is* a miracle that such an amazingly small number of Negro leaders (and blacks themselves) have turned Communist with what went on in this country over the last two hundred years. Strange as it might seem to a brainwashed America, even Paul Robeson wasn't a Communist. Yes, Paul went to Russia, but not because he believed in what they were doing as much as *not* being able to stand seeing what was going on in America.

Communist, Fascist, rightist—haven't they all become almost meaningless words, anyway? The question is: *Was Martin's cause just?* And who's to decide anyway? In a free society, is there any more immoral act than invading the rights of a citizen?

As I rather agonizingly watched person after person react wrongly to what was said about Martin Luther King, Jr., after his death, I caught a connection between *that* and the mentality that taps conversations in bedrooms. And, really, we can't expect to be rid of that mentality at the top until we deal with it at the root rung of the ladder—with those who are too holier-than-thou to stay dedicated to the best in a man when something less than the best is exposed, or with those who are too jaded or apathetic to be holier-than-thou. With *ourselves.* Because in almost every American I've known, sadly, there's something of Moe, Dorothy or Blue. Possibly I'm more sensitive to it because I've gone through the same. Maybe no one except Hitler hated me till *Blackthink*, but just about everybody *deserted* me more than once when I got into trouble before that.

In the early sixties, I failed to make sure my business managers were filing income tax returns for me. I'm not copping a plea—*I* must've been sick in the head to get so busy that I didn't check on a thing like that. But the biggest shock wasn't when the Internal Revenue man came to take me downtown. It was when my friends "took" me. And my "fans."

When the tax thing broke I was making my living the same way I had basically for twenty years: speaking to the young and doing things with them. I'd made speeches, had off-the-cuff raps, held youth clinics and set up gang-prevention centers all over the world. After I was indicted for failure to pay my income taxes, the requests kept coming in from Ghana and Germany, England and New Zealand, Peru and Israel.

But not from Iowa.

Or Harlem.

Or Alabama.

Or San Francisco.

Not from the civic groups anymore, or from the interracial groups, or interreligious groups. Not from the schools much, either—though I never saw one kid whose attitude toward me had changed.

I had trouble making a living. Thank God my three daughters were all grown and married.

Ruth and I pulled our belts in, moved out of the apartment in which we'd watched the girls grow to womanhood, took a smaller place and for months and months, no matter where I was—and now I often was traveling for fifty dollars and expenses, not five hundred dollars—waited not just to see if I would ever make a good living again, but whether I'd go to jail. Fortunately, when my case came up the judge wasn't as much of a Puritan as the National Conference of Christians and Jews or Moe and Dorothy.

Or the autograph hunters I met in the street. As I said, the kids never changed. But there was suddenly a new breed of adult. The worst were men in my age bracket. They walked up to me now with exaggerated aggressiveness because I wasn't only of their generation, I was like them in a lot of other ways. Did they dip into the petty cash at work? So what—I'd dipped into the big cash. Or so they thought.

But I still had my friends.

I had them for about four hours after the first story hit the Chicago papers.

I'd been home for one straight week, a long stretch for me. It was my final full day in town. I'd just left my P.R. firm (which went out of business because of the tax scandal), had set aside one last afternoon for golf. Joe Louis was in town, too. He was one of our foursome for that day. The other two were old buddies of mine.

I got back to the apartment just before noon, ate a sandwich while changing clothes. I was due to tee off at one. The phone rang and Ruth answered it in the other room.

"Jesse," she said, a minute later, "it was Frank. Said he couldn't make it. I asked him did he want to talk to you, but he said no, he was in a rush." There was a strange expression on her face. And on mine. Frank hadn't missed a golf date in years.

"What is it, Ruth?"

She brought the morning paper over to me. I hadn't had time to read it. "Did you see this, Jesse?"

I stared at the article she was pointing to. I'd known about my tax case for quite a while, of course. It was tearing my guts out. But I hadn't told anyone outside of my family.

"You can't think . . ."

"I do, Jesse," she said softly. "I'm afraid I *do*."

Ruth Owens is a remarkable woman. Remember the monkey who sees no evil, hears no evil and speaks no evil? He got the idea from my wife. She's like Joe Louis—with an education. If Ruth sensed that Frank had canceled out of our golf date because he'd read the paper and didn't want to be seen with me anymore, that had to be it.

I lost my temper. "Well, the son-of-a-bitch can go to hell!" I threw down my sandwich. "There're a thousand people I can call right now and they'd be at the tee in forty minutes." I walked to the phone. Before I could pick up the receiver, it rang.

It was the fourth member of our foursome. He couldn't make it. Out-of-town guest had just turned up. I said bring him. He said the guest didn't play golf.

I didn't play golf that day, either. I had Joe over to the house, drank a few drinks with him and told him my troubles, just as he'd told me his tax troubles years before. They'd deserted him like rats on a sinking ship, too, then.

That wasn't why Joe Louis didn't desert me, though. He—and a few others, *very* few outside of my family—stuck by during the worst because Joe is good people. All the others, not just the millions (and this sharecropper's son will never completely get over the fact that there actually *are* millions) who'd shaken my hand through the years, but the ones I'd seen socially copped out in one way or another. Sometimes it was subtle, maybe subconscious. Paul, my writing collaborator of fourteen years—who was born less than two years before I went to the Berlin Olympics—called me twice in the year before my case came to court. The second time was to tell me he would've called more, but things had really piled up on him during that year. They'd piled up on me, too.

I'm not putting Paul down—he's the "world's second fastest human." I'm sincerely sure that 98 percent of the reason he never even called just to ask, "How are you?" was because he was superbusy. In the years since I wrote *Blackthink,* I've gained quite a few insights about some pretty heavy-sounding things—like world peace, race prejudice, human rights. But nothing has changed *my* life more than seeing how being too busy can mean being less human.

As soon as I got the clue from the world, *I* started to back off. I took what work I could find. Ruth and I—instead of being wildly caught up in an endless string of obligations—sat alone those increasingly frequent nights when I was home, just talking. It was like the old times we never had, and if the threat of no more times together hadn't been hanging over my head, it would have been one of the best years of my life. When the day finally did come, I knew fear like I'd never known. But resolution, too, in a way.

That morning as I walked to the front door, she put her hand on me. "Are you prepared?" she asked softly.

"There's no way to prepare for this," I answered hoarsely. "I'll just have to take my medicine."

Because I was prepared even to go to jail, impossibly humiliating as that would have been. For in a way it wouldn't have been worse than what I'd already gone through. What good is it being on the outside if *that's* a jail, too?

As it turned out, I went "free." I'd never be free

again in some ways. Still, no matter what the world did to me, I never dreamed in my most insane nightmare that they'd do it to Martin.

Is Martin Luther King, Jr., really revered today? You can answer that by asking yourself how much his basic beliefs are being followed and how much he's just a comfortable memory to most blacks and whites.

We hear a lot of talk, for instance, about whether he was really "effective." Because there's hate in the world, does that mean Jesus Christ wasn't "effective"? "I got to call it as I see it," one black teacher said to me with a whole ton of intellectual honesty a few months ago. "Martin was outdated when he died. In a way, it was lucky for him that he went when he did."

I wanted to strangle that teacher.

But the man went on. "Case in point. When he came into Chicago in '66. Jesse, you said yourself that Martin was wrong in taking over the slum buildings and taking it upon himself to collect the rent."

"I thought he was," I answered with jaw set. "But he did it out of frustration. Mayor Daley didn't lift a hand to help him here."

The teacher kept on talking, but I couldn't take it. I excused myself and found his kids playing out in the yard. Yet I wasn't fit for even the young that evening. The anger in me had been replaced by a pervasive sickness. What in the hell was I doing defending Martin? Was that where things were at?

Frankly, I feel that way now. In the Alabama where I came from—and the slums of Cleveland afterward—defenses were a dime a dozen. The same went for the Olympics. And for working with kids after that, kids with fathers who were home one night of the week, kids whose mothers had seen every girl in the family turn into a prostitute and most of the boys heroin addicts before puberty. You worked with those kids and if they got on the straight and narrow, you didn't make any speeches about it. Because for each one you helped, you lost two. And when *they* went bad, you didn't cop any pleas.

Unless you were really there to *use* the kids, not understand them.

Like people *used* Martin's memory instead of understanding what he stood for. But talk is cheap in a world where Presidents make war and call themselves Quakers, where their highest placed men put microphones at bedroom keyholes with one hand and salute the flag with the other, where leading liberals inhumanly write a great man off because he was human and then ask whether it's "humanly possible" to do anything else.

Americans *used* Martin Luther King, Jr. They used him as an unapproachable god on earth so that they could get away with their own pettiness. Dorothy and Blue and Moe could afford to be the frailest, most compromising of people just as long as they were able to say, "Well, *no one* can ever be as good as Martin Luther King—he's a human saint."

I used those exact same words in my first book.

But the minute Martin became mortal, the minute America saw human anger in him when he lashed out at a white slumlord or saw the lust of the flesh in him and had to stop believing his four children were virgin births—then they hated him.

Yes, underneath it all, *hated*. While he was a saint, you could pay your dues and forget it. When he became human, *they* could be measured against him.

The overwhelming majority of people in this country, black and white alike, haven't grown up. They don't really want leaders. They want idols—impossible things that don't move their bowels or have underarm odor or adulterous impulses.

Once they discovered they've made a mistake, they'll tear the whole beautiful body and soul to shreds to cover the feet of clay.

Dear Gloria, Beverly, Marlene—

You're all in your thirties now.

I'm almost sixty.

When you were little girls, I used to say how you—and your mother—were my "four *real* gold medals." But now you're no longer little girls, and I've finally stopped thinking of you as medals for your father.

Yet I feel I treasure you the more. Your colors are no longer gold to me—but black and red and silver, for what you are as unique human beings. I never dreamed when you were wearing identical dresses and hair ribbons that you'd turn out so very differently from each other—and from me. But your differences have shown me the incomparable value and beauty of human differences better than all else.

Your Father

There was one thing even worse than seeing people desert me. Traveling hundreds of millions of miles and speaking to hundreds of millions of people over thirty years had brainwashed me to think not just that all people liked me, but that they all liked me for pretty much the same reason.

I always talked a good game where human differences were concerned.

I couldn't really *play* the game, though, because human differences and human conflicts *didn't* exist for *me*. Oh, I knew they "existed." But the differences between Jesse Owens and other people hadn't changed anything in *my* life. No one wanted to come into conflict with me. Hitler had been the rare exception. Only a memory now. And I'd defeated him. It had made the color of my skin—and anything else that was different about me—matter even less.

My home life was the epitome of that.

After I came home from the 1936 Olympics with my four medals, it became increasingly apparent that everyone was going to slap me on the back, want to shake my hand or have me up to their suite. But no one was going to offer me a job.

I'd gotten together some money by forsaking my amateur status and, after working at the sometimes enjoyable but basically humiliating job as maintenance man and children's instructor at a Cleveland playground (for thirty dollars a week), finally went into Negro baseball and made a few bucks. Soon after, a couple of white promoters came along and offered me a chain of cleaning stores with my name on them. I put every penny I had into it, and woke up one morning to no partners and bankruptcy.

It was becoming glaringly obvious to me that the only way Jesse Owens could make a living in a world that didn't allow blacks into its professional sports or any of its important jobs was to tread on my past fame. That meant traveling. And travel I did. From one end of the country to the other, soon from one end of the globe to the other. Ruth often said that being married to me "wasn't like having a husband. It was like having a boyfriend." There were times when I was home that seldom.

With that kind of situation, most wives would have either gotten a lover, a divorce or a job. Ruth found a fourth alternative. She became a full-time mother as few mothers have. She held our family together not with the cheap glue on the back of suitcase travel stickers, but with the unseverable arteries of her heart. She raised those three girls just like any kids whose dad walked in the front door at six every night.

Yet she didn't fake it, either. It was obvious I *wasn't* walking in that front door every night or even most nights—sometimes only once a month. So she made my coming home not only a relaxing time for me where I could immerse myself into a warm, loving family unit and regain what people often took from me, but she made an *event* out of it, too.

I don't think I ever once walked through that door in all those years—unless I'd taken an early plane and the girls were in school—when the three of them weren't waiting in their party dresses and hair ribbons to leap into my arms. When there were only four, Ruth kept the unity of five somehow so that when I was home, it was as if nothing had changed. I of course recall those few but treasured times when all of us *were* together for weeks at a stretch, like the time we drove from Detroit to Cleveland with Ruth and me in the front and Gloria, Beverly and Marlene in the back singing "I've Been Working on the Railroad" and "Row, Row, Row Your Boat."

But much more often I remember *coming* home, especially when I returned from tours of the world. There was one time in particular. We weren't doing well at all that year—I was still paying off from the Jesse Owens Cleaners fiasco—yet, as always, Ruth had found a way to put together a royal dinner and to dress the girls out in frilly, feminine new-looking clothes. But when I walked in, there were only three to greet me.

"Where's Marlene?" I asked.

"I don't know for sure," Ruth said. I sensed at once that six-year-old Marlene had done something bad, but that Ruth didn't want to tell on her.

"How about a hint?" I said, after I'd kissed Ruth and the two older girls.

"She might just possibly be out in the backyard hiding, Dad," Gloria whispered.

I went out into the yard. Marlene was flat to the ground behind the farthest clump of bushes, dug in like a soldier.

"C'mon out, Marlene honey!" I called. "What's the matter?"

Slowly, she made her way out of the hiding place. "I did a cartwheel in the living room, Daddy," she said meekly.

"And?" I tried to keep from smiling.

"And . . . I broke Mommy's favorite lamp. Didn't you see it was missing?"

"Come *here*," I told her, holding out my arms. She raced up into them, smothering me with hugs and kisses.

How could I have come home after more than a month and chastised her? I couldn't have spanked her. Sometimes, though not often, the girls did things a lot worse than breaking Ruth's favorite lamp, and I'd always give them a good lecture for it. But I could never lay a hand on them. It just wasn't in me.

"Tell you what, Marlene honey," I said to her as we walked toward the house that day. "Daddy can't be home this Christmas. He's going to be in a faraway place called Afghanistan. But he'll bring you a doll back from there if you don't do any more cartwheels in the living room."

"Oh, Daddy, that would be wonderful!" Marlene

squealed. "I'll never do another cartwheel there, I promise!"

And she never did.

We entered the house, holding hands. That January I brought her back a doll from Afghanistan. Every Christmas after until she was almost a grown woman, I had a new doll for her from some foreign country: Ireland, Malaysia, India—lots of others.

So maybe we didn't always have Christmas together, but we always had Christmas.

And that was why, from the beginning, I called Ruth and the three girls "my four gold medals." Whatever compliments, tributes, applause and hero-worship I received from the world those two hundred fifty plus days a year I was away were like the artificial light of a photographer's studio next to the bright spring sun of what I had waiting for me at home. "I have three fine daughters and a wonderful wife," I'd say to myself when the loneliness got too bad. And it was true. Yet to me, they were all cut from the same fine cloth, too, a tapestry of silk but also of sameness. As the years passed, as three distinctly different personalities began subtly but surely to emerge from Gloria, Beverly and Marlene, I hardly noticed. Was it because I wasn't there enough to notice? Or was it something else? When I *was* there, was I playing a role that no longer always fit the scene?

As I look back on my first book—which was supposed to be the story of my life—it shocks me that I felt the most important things to say about my daughters were when they were born. *Blackthink* was written three years ago—when Marlene was almost thirty, Beverly already past that important number, and Gloria almost thirty-five.

* * *

After a father sees his children grow up, sees his daughters seriously date or go off to college or get ready to make their way in the world, it changes him. Most men look in the mirror, see the wrinkles, maybe a pot belly and some gray hair, realize that they've been slowing up little by little.

Not me.

I had my kids young but, more than that, I was one of those people whom nature had allowed to escape the obvious signs of age—in a way let me escape age itself as I moved into my forties and my daughters out of their teens. Yes, I escaped *that* just as I escaped the very drastic change kids make for a man: sobering responsibilities, a new, stabler kind of existence centered around the home.

The big change that Gloria, Beverly and Marlene made in my life—that *they* had changed—came just last year.

I surely *should* have started to see it, of course, when Beverly eloped in 1957—started to see how "kids" become human beings. Deeply different human beings. Human beings you can learn from.

I was home for what I hoped would be a relatively quiet three days. Beverly was home from college on vacation. I heard her say to her mother, "Where's Daddy?"

"I think he's in the den," Ruth answered.

"You'd better get him."

Ruth walked into the den and together we went to the living room with Beverly. I knew *something* was up, but I never dreamed she'd say, "Daddy—Mommy —I'm married!"

She was still in her teens. Ruth and I had been a good deal younger when we eloped. But I'd forgotten that, I guess. So I just stood there in shock for a minute. Finally, I snapped out of it and took her into my arms. "Where's the lucky man, hon?" I asked her. He was waiting outside, of course!

Still, seeing my daughters all married within a period of a few years wasn't a real shock. I expected, wanted them to marry, and they all found good men.

It was nice and tidy. So what if *they* were getting older. *I* wasn't. The only trouble with that was the world—*it* wasn't nice and tidy anymore. And my girls and their husbands were starting to react to the world, each in their own unique way. As the years passed, as they neared or became thirty and I became fifty, the individual personalities they'd really had for so long burst forth.

Gloria's change was the first to confront me, not only because she was the eldest, but because she challenged some of my basic beliefs. Gloria was the young adult of the sixties, old enough not to want to bomb buildings—because they might fall on her very own children—but young enough to know that things *must* change and *now*. She'd earned an M.A. in education "because these black kids have to be taught," working within the system only for that reason while hating the schools she had to teach in, schools where the entrance halls for the world to see were beautiful and the insides for the kids to learn were snake pits. With her husband, Malcolm Hemphill, the assistant principal of Chicago's largest high school, Gloria worked tirelessly, becoming more and more militant without becoming a cynic. For to her, the kids of today—the ones who call her "mother" *and* the ones who call her "teacher"—are more alive, more aware than any kids, any adults ever have been. She and Hemp, and a group of others like them, are working on what they call an "Alternative System of Education" that could someday be a model for every city across the country.

I don't agree with every detail of it, just as I still don't agree with the "America the Ugly" attitude secretly held by many of the 1968 American Olympic athletes, according to Hemp.

But I respect my eldest daughter and her husband. Deeply. And as often as not, I've learned to see what they're about. They've changed me.

Beverly turned out to be a rebel of a different kind. If Gloria threw aside the old politics, Beverly scoffed at old-fashioned social conventions. She was the one I caught smoking in her room, the one who still shocks her mother.

Yet if she plays hard, Beverly works just as hard. Her husband, Donald Prather, is also an assistant principal, and Beverly is in black education, as well as being active within several important organizations. But she has never let the fact that she's "Jesse Owens' daughter" stop her from doing what she likes. So she's made mistakes, but never the one biggest mistake of not having a good heart. Some people say she's the most like me of the three. Recently when I got mad at her for something, she won me over by looking straight at me and saying, "Daddy, maybe I was wrong. But *you* were the one who told me years ago: 'No matter what you do, Bev—even if it's wrong—do it *well.*' "

It's impossible not to love a girl like that. And because Beverly's openness as a human being, her childlike love of life, is even greater than mine, she's a constant lesson to me as to how good, so good, life really is.

Marlene is my baby, though right now she's twelve years older than I was when I went to the Berlin

Olympics, and she's as different from the other two girls as they are from each other. A social worker writing poverty programs for the federal government with a husband, Stuart Rankin, who's an advertising executive, Marlene cuts through all hypocrisies, yet somehow does it with charm and femininity. I was as proud as I could be, for instance, when she became the first black Homecoming Queen at my alma mater, Ohio State. But after graciously accepting the award, Marlene turned quietly to me and said, "Paula should have won it, really. She's prettier than I am. If I hadn't been black or Jesse Owens' daughter, I think Paula would have been Homecoming Queen." And after Stuart landed an account-executive position with probably the most important ad agency in the world, Leo Burnett & Company, which had been reputed to be prejudiced against blacks and Jews, Ruth and I had them over for a celebration dinner as soon as I got back into town.

"How did he pull *that* off?" I asked Marlene.

"Well, let's face it, Dad," she said. "For one thing, Stuart is very light. I mean, he's good, awfully good. But that wouldn't have been any help if he'd been a *black* black man."

I've always tried to be honest, but this kind of frankness was new to me. Yet it always comes out beautiful when Marlene says it, because Marlene is a beautiful person. And beauty—true beauty—always changes everyone it touches. For the better.

I couldn't see all the inner beauty of all three of my daughters for too long, because I had been partly blinded to the changes which had taken place inside them. I really believe I have always loved those girls as much as any father ever loved his daughters. But there has to be more than love. The gold medals of the thirties are sometimes so much dead weight in the seventies.

The frilly, simple, similar three children of my own thirties are gone forever—if indeed they were ever there. These married daughters of mine are not just bigger, older versions of the girls who sang "Row, Row, Row Your Boat" in the back of a car. They are different people, new people, the people of today. And tomorrow.

Facing *that* may have been harder for me than facing anything else. Because for one thing, it means I'm *not* thirty anymore.

But if I have to be sixty, then thank God *I've* changed, too.

Joe Louis
Los Angeles, California

Dear Joe—

You changed me most of all.

Jess

A cruel remark in a barber shop, hate letters, a book filled with love, the realization not only that my daughters had grown up but that they'd grown into much more than "daughters"—these were the first stinging jabs and then the resounding body blows to a part of me that hadn't changed in maybe fifty years.

But the knockout punch that brought me to my knees was thrown by my closest friend. Joe Louis.

Joe—who never threw a punch *outside* the ring.

Joe—who spent his life gladly letting people walk all over him, praying every minute that they wouldn't stumble and scuff their shoes.

Joe—the one argument, the one final, irrefutable, unbending argument that a black man could take it all, all the hate and abuse and oppression the white man had to give, and still have a wide smile, the widest, for the world. The whole world.

Yes, Martin Luther King preached nonviolence and benevolence toward his fellow man. Joe Louis never had to say a word. He *was*, more than Martin, more than anyone, nonviolence and benevolence.

Remember Lou Gehrig at that Yankee Stadium ceremony they held for him in the last months of his life, lateral amyotrophic sclerosis having brought him from a muscular two-hundred pounder who'd never missed a baseball game in his career to a weakened shadow of a man who couldn't hold a coffee cup? Remember when he steadied himself with the microphone as he poignantly said into it, "Today I consider myself the luckiest man on earth"?

Well, for my money, Joe Louis went Lou Gehrig even one better. Joe *didn't* die. No, he smilingly stayed around for the one torture even worse: a living death.

Joseph Louis Barrow came from the concentration camps of Alabama less than a year after I did. We never knew each other there, just as thousands upon thousands of slave families—and that's just what they were, *slaves*—hardly knew anyone except the white man who owned them. And *that* from a distance.

But Joe and I had one other thing in common besides age and Alabama: Nature had gifted us with unique physical attributes. Not that a lot of other Negroes in the South didn't have those same attributes to start with, but their bodies were soon wasted and broken by the sharecropping life. You started at six. If you got that far. More than half the babies died at birth—as both Joe and I almost did, as two brothers and one sister of mine did.

The difference was that Joe and I were both able to get out of the South. That was the one option our parents had had that made them different from the slaves in Abraham Lincoln's time. After working all his life and producing more for the white sharecropper than anyone else had for a hundred miles in any direction, in 1920 my father sold everything to the white man for twenty-four dollars and moved us all up to Cleveland. We knew we'd probably starve up there, too—and we almost did—but my parents figured anything was better than Alabama.

Joe escaped the horror of the South, too; his body survived, then grew big and strong with reflexes like few men have ever had. People called Joe dumb, because he hardly had any education, but we'll never know the truth since whatever possibilities Joe had to develop mentally were crushed in order that he could survive physically. Just as I found out I'd have to run my ass off to leave the ghetto, Joe found out early that the only way *he* could ever get a little bit more than near-starvation wages in the white world was to beat up other men inside a ring.

That was as far from Joe Louis's nature as Hitler was from being a libertarian. Not you, not I, not anyone would ever have known the name of Joe Louis if he'd been left on his own. But the minute the white promoters got a whiff of Joe L. Barrow's ability, his fate was sealed. Before he was old enough to vote, he'd taken the Golden Gloves Championship, turned pro the same year and won his first fight by a knockout in the first round. They pushed Joe hard after that, but he could take it. Then. Once he fought three times in a week, KO'ing every opponent. When he'd just turned twenty-three, he KO'd Jimmy Braddock and became World's Heavyweight Champion—the only Negro to do it since Jack Johnson decades before.

They pushed Joe even harder *after* he became champion. He defended his crown more often than our last half-dozen heavyweight titleholders put together. He *had to.* Because Joe Louis didn't have any money. He knew as much about money management as I knew about the cleaning business. He grossed five million dollars in pre-inflation days, yet was constantly asking his managers for handouts. Of course, there was another reason, too. Joe was the world's softest touch. I recall how after one fight the world was slapping him on the back and shaking his hand, how reporters couldn't get enough of him until 3:30 in the morning, and how after it was all through he turned to one of his handlers, sheepishly took out an empty wallet, I mean *absolutely empty,* and asked for meal money.

Five ten-dollar bills were peeled off a roll that would have fit Nelson Rockefeller's pocket, and Joe and I and a couple of other guys left for a little more revelry. Outside the building, an old black fighter was sitting beside a shoeshine kit. He was there because he had no place else to go.

"Shine, Champ?"

"Sure," Joe answered. We stood there for ten minutes while the graying, half-blind middleweight worked over Joe's shoes like they were jewels on a king's crown. Finally the rag and polish were put away. The ex-pug straightened up as much as he could and looked at Joe, smiling with his gums, that one eye a blank.

Joe didn't take out his small change. He took out his wallet. "How's it been goin', Sammy?" he asked as he did it.

"Oh, you know, Joe," the broken man answered with as much pride as he could muster. "Sometimes good, sometimes not so good."

"Well, you take care," Joe told him, stuffing four of the five tens into the gnarled hand.

I could tell you hundreds of stories like that—I mean *hundreds.* And for every one *I've* got to tell, there are dozens, maybe hundreds more. But I'm not as interested in telling you what Joe did for others as telling you what they did for him.

Remember that great scene between Rod Steiger and Marlon Brando in *On the Waterfront?* "You should have looked out for me, Joey," Brando says pathetically to Steiger after he's lost everything. "I was your kid brother."

Joe was everybody's "brother"—when *they* needed *him.* So he fought until he couldn't fight any more, and then he made a "comeback" because it was either that or be back where he started, and, when that inevitably failed, he went into wrestling and had a broken rib put through his heart so that finally he had to quit the world of sports or quit living.

Then Joe Louis retired. After that, though, they still used his name even if they couldn't use his body—on products, mainly. Most of the time he didn't get a penny from it. They still paid him a C or two now and then to walk into the ring at championship fights. And the strange thing—only it didn't seem strange if you knew Joe Louis—was that he walked into those rings with a genuine smile on his aging face. "He's still the same old Joe Louis," I heard someone say at a Floyd Patterson fight. Yeah, Joe still felt the world was a great place to live in and that he was the luckiest man alive.

And because it was Joe Louis, you believed it, even though it didn't seem possible.

Well, it *wasn't* possible.

Joe Louis Barrow ended up in a mental hospital. The papers made a big thing about it, but no one wrote a word about what put him there. It's about time someone did.

Maybe you're asking yourself a question right now,

though: *How come Jesse Owens is here to talk about it?* One answer is that the sport I was fit for was consistent with going to college and *not* becoming a professional athlete. Because of that, I got an education, and *didn't* make a million dollars. Joe was able to go almost straight from grammar school into prize-fighting. He was able to owe the government over a million in taxes, while I had to pay "only" $100,000 in all.

Actually, I did go into professional sports. Not too many people remember Negro baseball. I can never forget it. Most Americans over thirty know that until Jackie Robinson was fastballed into the major leagues by a brave Branch Rickey in 1947, there were no black athletes in baseball.

But there were black baseball players. They played for three dollars a night in their own leagues. Satchel Paige is one name you no doubt recognize. He didn't get into the majors until he was forty-five years old.

I went into Negro ball because I hadn't been able to make a living with my athletic prowess any other way, and my degree from Ohio State hadn't gotten me anything better than playground instructor. When the white promoters (they owned Negro baseball, too, where it was worth owning) came and said they didn't want me to play, but to capitalize on my Olympic medals by putting on an "exhibition" against a thoroughbred racehorse before the game, I balked. When they said the exhibition might make me a hundred bucks a night, I went for it. I never hit or caught a baseball. I raced against an animal—*another* animal.

Because, finally, I realized that an exhibition—a disgraceful exhibition—was just what I'd been putting on. The worst part wasn't racing a hundred yards against a horse.

It was that the "race" was rigged.

How could a man ever beat a thoroughbred horse when the fastest a human had run a mile then wasn't even four minutes? Horses did it way under two minutes. But I never lost. Because the starter held the gun near the horse's ear. The poor animal would be so frightened that I'd be thirty yards ahead before he got started. Sure, he'd be streaking by me just after the finish line—but not until I reached it. The promoters had it figured out to the inch.

The fans never figured it out, though. Or maybe they didn't care. They got their thrill—"watching Jesse Owens outdo what he'd done to Hitler by miraculously beating a racehorse," as one promo said. And I got my money.

It makes me sick now even to think of it.

But I did it. I did it for almost a year.

Then one day I couldn't do it anymore. There was just no hiding it from myself one minute longer.

I was the animal.

The horse had retained its dignity.

I've been taken a lot of times since. But after that year, I never let myself be *used.* Except maybe by Jesse Owens.

Joe Louis wasn't so lucky. They not only took him to the cleaners, they put him through the washer until his color was nearly gone. I began to notice the change in a Birmingham hotel room in January of 1970.

Not that there hadn't been signs the last few times Joe and I had been together. But then we've been together off and on since the 1930's when those two Germans named Schmeling and Hitler had turned a spotlight on both of us that was never to be turned off, and I guess there've been a few times when I'd acted flaky in Joe's eyes, too. It never stopped us from being close, closer than even brothers can be, because it was as if we'd been the only two of our kind for a long, long time. It would've been lonesome as hell without knowing there was at least that one other.

There was a night in 1939, for instance, when Joe figured I'd flipped a little. It was after he'd fought Tony Galento. We'd gone to maybe twelve, fifteen parties for Joe at just about every plush hotel in Manhattan. The last and lushest was the penthouse suite of a white billionaire whose seven corporations didn't employ a single Negro.

Not even as janitor.

The guy was patting Joe on the back for about the fiftieth time with his lily-white hand when I exploded. "You wouldn't let him in the back door of one of your factories if he wasn't Heavyweight Champion!"

I apologized but left the party. As I was going down the hall, Joe caught up with me. "Don't you leave on account of me, Joe," I told him.

"Aw, it wasn't much of a party, anyway," he said. "But why'd you get mad?"

I looked into his guileless eyes. "Because you let these guys *use* you."

He looked at me, bewildered. "They aren't using me, Jesse," he said. "They're my *friends*."

I shook my head—but suddenly more at myself than at Joe. If he could go through life with that feeling, how could he ever be hurt?

I began to find out in that Birmingham room. Until then Joe Louis had been the one last rebuttal against the extreme militants, the one Rock of Gibraltar for every black who was willing to work within the system. "I can't keep on taking it—it's not humanly possible!" I'd heard time and time again through the years, whether I was talking to forty-year-old cabdrivers or fourteen-year-old gang members.

I'd heard it from myself, too. But I'd taken it. By saying to myself what I'd said to them: "It *is* possible. Look at Joe Louis."

But in January of 1970, when I looked at Joe Louis across that room in, ironically, Alabama, all the suppressed dread of dozens of years welled up in me at once and threatened to break out.

He wasn't the same Joe.

His mind would wander, he—who'd known no equal in the ring for twelve incredible years—had physical fears which most people walking out on the street below that hotel room never had.

There are gorier details, but I won't go into those. It's enough to say that four months later Joe Louis was hospitalized in a Veterans Administration hospital in Denver. The day I heard that was one of the worst —if not the worst—of my life.

For Joe Louis didn't get put in that hospital from any brain damage he'd suffered as a fighter. I knew *that* from the beginning. Tests proved it out later. Joe Louis was put in that hospital from *soul damage.* The heels of the shoes that had walked over him had finally dug in too deep. The years of always turning the other cheek, of having to ask for meal money and pleading with his government not to put him in jail when the millions he'd given away left him impossibly in debt, of watching young blacks deserting him as an Uncle Tom while older blacks and whites simply forgot him because he wasn't satisfying their racism or blood lust anymore—added up, up, *up* till they finally inevitably tipped the emotional scales even for Joe Louis.

If he'd had a speck less goodness and naïveté in

him, he would've seen what had been done to him for what it was, would've seen the world around him for what it sometimes is, and never would have found himself where he did a couple of years ago.

I knew there was evil out there, only I thought it could be overcome. Joe Louis couldn't countenance evil at all, couldn't understand that it even existed. When it was so tight around him that he was almost suffocating with it, the only way he had left to deal with it was simply not to face it—not to face reality—at all for a while. His being put in the hospital really wasn't a testament to his being sick, but to his incredibly vulnerable beauty.

Today, of course, Joe is long gone from the hospital. And he's pretty much the same Joe. Pretty much.

But make no mistake. The lightning combinations, the sleek, rippling brown muscles, are no longer there. Joe can be hit at will now, and every punch, every kick when he's down—in a world where no ref counts over you and stops them at ten—will take a crucial toll.

Like yours truly, Joseph Louis Barrow is almost sixty years old, too. And, no matter what *he* thinks, he's *not* the luckiest man in the world. Joe Louis is down. Joe, the sweetest, most beautiful thing you ever had, America, is hurt. Hurt *bad.*

I know—*you* didn't do it. You didn't even know about it. How could you?

You were always looking the other way when it was happening.

WHAT THAT CHANGE MEANS

Andy H.
A Suburb of Chicago

Dear Andy:

I've given a lot of thought to your question and decided on a different answer. Yes, Andy, "all that winning" finally *did* become boring.

Jesse Owens

Obviously, the change that took place in me had to spell changes in my daily life. But mostly they were subtle ones.

I found myself not willing, for example, to make even the best of my speeches over and over, wanted to say something new, even if it was only translating an experience I'd had that same day into some mutual meaning for a new bunch of youngsters. Creating sweeping "new" concepts like "immoderate moderate" had begun to seem like *kid* stuff next to that. I discovered, too, that I wasn't taking quite as much pride in being "the world's fastest human." I still didn't want to slow up physically—I'd rather die than get old—but if I was able to go forty-five minutes on the basketball court with fellows half my age or shoot in the high seventies even though I was almost sixty, I didn't feel as much of a compulsion to run, run, run off the court or the course.

Little things. Gradual things. Were they adding up

to much? I wasn't sure. I knew some of my *ideas* had changed a lot. But unless something deeper has been transformed inside a man, his ideas can change every Friday night.

Time passed. More time. One day I deliberately took off an afternoon to do nothing. Absolutely nothing. I found myself in our den, writing years-overdue letters to old friends, reading over parts of a couple of books, putting some of my scrapbooks in order. When I came to a 1935 photo of myself and Ralph Metcalfe, I started to see what that change had meant.

Ralph—a black man who these days is the second most powerful figure in Chicago politics—was a junior at Ohio State when I entered. At the time, he was the best sprinter in the country, had barely missed a gold medal at the 1932 Olympics. Even though he was pointing toward the 1936 Games so he could achieve that dream, he took me under his wing as much as any of my brothers ever did, helped me with personal problems as well as the one out on the field.

When I write that Ralph Metcalfe was the greatest sprinter of his day, I'm sure most of you will draw a blank. But he was—the best.

Me included.

Ralph was tall, yet powerful, with legs longer and more heavily muscled than mine, a chest with more lung capacity. Like Bob Hayes, the most recent "world's fastest human," Ralph possessed that rare body which fused the ultimate in power with a stunning speed. What's more, he owned that rare willpower to drive his body to its mental and physical limits.

Ralph had only one drawback, in fact: the Greeks and Romans had played a dirty trick on him. They'd arbitrarily made the dashes one hundred and two hundred meters, because those were nice round figures. In America, we did the same, except with yards instead of meters. Even then, the powers-that-be sensed that two hundred yards was too short for a *real* sprint, so they made it two-twenty. It wasn't enough. Today we look upon the four-forty and even eight-eighty as dashes. If Ralph were running *those* today, he'd be beyond belief. Why didn't he run them then? Because black men never ran anything longer than the dashes. Any race longer took luxuries like real tracks, not sidewalks or school halls.

He had trouble—as much as any champion can have "trouble"—with the two-twenty and especially the hundred. He was too powerful, his body too good, so it took him a second to really get moving. I was built closer to the ground—with smaller feet, for example, which could zoom away—so I always got off ahead of Ralph, and, in the shorter dash, was able to keep that lead even though he invariably was but a breath behind me at the end.

The two-twenty was tougher. There, Ralph was a breath ahead of me often as not. In a two-fifty or three-hundred-yard dash, he would always have been first. His superpowerful body never let up, his competitive fierceness—which was almost shocking in a man with such brotherly kindness off the track—let you know he was never going to quit, *never*, that those long-striding, heavier steps which kept coming closer and closer, louder and louder, behind you, would never quit, were going to wear you the hell down if it was the last thing they did. In every two-twenty I ran against Ralph Metcalfe, he was *always* ahead of me those couple of yards after the finish line when you're still going your fastest out of pure momentum. But I was lucky enough, much of the time, to get to that finish line first.

As in the 1936 Olympics. Ralph was a little past his peak there. I was right at mine. And it was because of those Olympics that hardly anyone remembers Ralph for what he did in the earlier thirties—though an awful lot of people seem to know him for what he's doing now.

But I remember—and I see, finally, the connection between *then* and *now*.

I remember first going against Ralph in 1933 at the National A.A.U. It had been just about three weeks before, on a Friday afternoon, that I'd been able to set the world record in the hundred. Fantastic competitor that he was, Ralph equaled the record that very same night!

Naturally, both of us couldn't win in the A.A.U. There was a tremendous air of excitement, second only to the Olympics, as we got ready for that race. Ralph was the established champion, our best bet for the Games in Berlin—a celebrity-plus among athletes. I'd just become a different kind of celebrity—I was still in high school!

I'll never forget that race. It might have been my best. I got off to a fantastic start—you knew from his reputation that you had to get off to a fantastic start and be ahead of Ralph because, if you were ever even with him or behind him, you were a sure loser.

He was almost a full stride behind at the thirty-yard marker. I could sense it by the sounds in back of me. The other sounds were relatively dim. It was a race between him and me.

As we passed the halfway mark, the Metcalfe sounds got louder. I'd always run soft, been taught by Charles

Riley to run as if I were dancing on hot coals. But Ralph hit the turf like a racehorse.

A thoroughbred.

With twenty yards to go I could see him out of the corner of my eye. The margin wasn't a yard anymore. It was a foot. As the finish line loomed up before us, the foot was an inch. But I had him—I had him—I was so near—so damn close—

I hit the tape and for the first time in as long as I could remember, it had *too* much give.

I hadn't hit it first.

On my right, like a locomotive at its top speed, big Ralph had passed me, an inch in front.

I got myself together as much as possible and went over to congratulate him. He knew how I felt. "Good race, guy," he gasped, still out of breath.

I was gasping, too. But not *quite* as much as he was. "I thought I *had* you," I said honestly.

He grinned, put a hand on my shoulder. "Maybe that's what beat you, Jesse," he said, and walked away. It took me thirty odd years to learn the wisdom of his remark. For that night all I could think of was the next time I'd be racing Ralph Metcalfe. Beating him would be everything. An extra reason I'd wanted to go to Ohio State so much was to run against Ralph.

We competed a lot after that. We'd both tied the world's record that day at the A.A.U., and kept on battering at it as hard as we battered at each other. Every race was the same script: I'd be off to a lightning start, he'd wear me down at the end. The question was whether he'd wear me down in time.

In the hundred, he usually didn't. In the 220, he often did. As a matter of fact, our competition stood at that slightest of margins—me ahead by just one—when the 1936 Olympics arrived. Ralph had already graduated college, was a little slower than usual working his powerful frame into shape. He didn't quite have the stuff to beat me in either the hundred or two hundred meters at Berlin.

The race I remember most where he was concerned, though, took place after the Games. We'd gone down to Cologne for a hundred-meter exhibition. I figured it'd be a breeze. After the gun went off and I'd left the starting holes way in front of everyone else, it looked like I was right. The pressure was off; the confrontation with Hitler was over. I'd won my four gold medals. This was just going to be the icing on the cake.

I think I got off to a better lead over Ralph that day than I ever had. I was absolutely relaxed, which was when I ran my best. My body was gliding seemingly without effort in the "picture runner" style people said I had. After thirty yards, I could hardly even hear Ralph behind me.

I turned it on even more.

I felt like my feet weren't even touching the ground.

I was *flying*.

In that moment I had everything. I was really going to make *this* icing something to remember. I was going to tie my world's record, damn it!

One official caught the winning time in a new world's record that day, but the other two said that the old record had been tied, so that's how it was put in the books.

I wasn't the winner, though. I'd come in second. At the halfway mark, I'd heard those familiar, pounding footsteps. I wasn't worried. The finish line seemed just a few feet away. But it wasn't. I never knew that better than I did with ten yards left, never knew it better than when Ralph Metcalfe's tall figure loomed at my side, his right elbow almost touching my left one.

I turned on even *more.*

And so did *he.*

The tape exploded before us like a grenade. I held my breath for the last two strides, gave it my very life, lunged.

And that beautiful son-of-a-bitch lunged a little farther!

What a champion! I thought to myself as I threw my arms around him, as much for support as for congratulations. This was true greatness. Ralph cared just as much about an exhibition in Cologne as he had about the Olympic Games in Berlin.

That unique kind of integrity—which is different from merely being honest—was what allowed him to leave the world of sports for a more real, adult world, while I was too often retreading my footsteps of those adolescent years. One day it would make him the most important black man in Chicago. Whether or not I agree a hundred percent with his politics, that's a hell of an accomplishment.

Though it took me thirty-five years to sort it out, the message of Ralph Metcalfe was this: The minute you think you've got it beaten, *you're* beaten. No matter what you did yesterday, each sunrise wipes the slate clean. In *Blackthink,* I said that manhood has to be earned. Well, it has to be earned anew *every day.*

Another insight my competition with Ralph finally awakened in me is that life is no sprint. It's a marathon—a long, long, long-distance race over hills and through valleys, sometimes even with stops along the way, and it's how you run that marathon, not how soon you get to the finish line, that matters. Because there really is no finish line. As long as you live, there's another hill, another valley.

Of course, to be painfully honest, I'm not a whole long way from the end of *my* race. I'm almost sixty years old. My mother and father died before the Second World War. Most of my brothers and sisters are gone. Soon I'll have a forty-year-old daughter. Yes, most of my race has been run, and there's no doing it over a second time. No matter what I say in this book that may be born of a new openness, a lot of people will answer: "Just another establishment Negro moving a little to the left," or "One more Uncle Tom a generation late and a revolution short!"

In a way, it's true. For no matter what I say here, this book must finally reaffirm certain old values, the ones that—through all my own deep changes—I've seen tested and retested and have never come up wanting for me. I'm no iconoclast, no innovator, no philosopher. I'm only someone who had a unique pair of legs and maybe a little extra drive to go with them, an essentially ordinary man trying to make sense of the experiences of my life and what's going on around me. I've still got more questions than answers. One reason I had some of the wrong answers was that for many years, unfortunately, some of the *wrong* answers worked for me.

One of the moments when I felt that most keenly was the spring weekend I drove out to Paul's to do part of the taping for this book. We were sitting out in front of his house when some neighborhood kids recognized me, started coming over. After they'd gotten their autographs and athletic advice, we were alone again—except for one boy, Andy. "I read your book, Mr. Owens," he said, meaning my children's autobiography. "It was real good. Except for one thing."

"What's that?" I asked.

"Well . . ." he hesitated.

"Go ahead, Andy," I encouraged. "You're among friends."

"Okay," he answered. "It was *all that winning.* I mean—you never did anything but win, Jesse. To be honest, it got a little boring after awhile. Didn't it ever get boring for you?"

I laughed out loud. "Believe it or not, it *didn't,*" I told him.

When he was gone and we were alone again, I turned to Paul. Suddenly I wasn't laughing or smiling anymore.

"Did I ever tell you what Mel Walker once said to Ruth about me?" Mel, a fine athlete, had been even closer to me in college than Ralph Metcalfe had.

Paul shook his head.

"Mel told her: 'Ruth, Jesse only made one mistake in his entire life—he never lost when it really meant something.' "

A. S. "Doc" Young
c/o *The New York Times*
New York, N. Y.

Dear Doc:

When you reviewed my first book for the *Times*, you made some points that only a wise old head like yourself could make. Like how the blackthinkers claim all the "positives" for themselves when really a lot of Negroes worked a lot of years so that people like James Meredith could march and the Stokely Carmichaels could shout about it. You even brought a tear to an eye that has seen more than a little itself, when you said that Harry Edwards—who called me a "bootlicking Uncle Tom"—"is a beneficiary of a Jesse Owens who, during his fifty-seven years, has had a thousand good reasons for giving up but who never did." That glamorized me more than I deserved, Doc, but otherwise I agreed with almost everything you said.

And still do—except for your idea that it was beneath my dignity to "spend so much time and thought on guys who never could have carried his water bucket" and that "it's long past time when the other side should be heard at full strength."

I'm partly on "the other side" now, Doc. What about *you?* We've both been around a long time in this struggle. You wrote your review two years ago, I wrote the book three years back. I'm not just throwing the bouquet back when I say *you* and those like you have done much more to lay the foundation for the Merediths and Malcolms than I. But I've also come to see that a lot of them—an awful lot—can more than carry my water bucket, just as quite a few have picked up your pen. I don't think it's at all beneath our dignity to talk about them. I think our dignity and integrity depend in large part on helping them where we agree they've got something. Because *they're* where it's at, Doc.

Warmly,
Jesse

For several years I've held a position with the American League in spring training teaching baseball players how to run correctly. Last time, former black pitching great Don Newcombe was around for a while and we traded stories.

"Did I ever tell you the time I had to give an order to a black guy five feet five who weighed about a hundred and twenty pounds?" Newk asked. Newk, by the way, stands six four and weighs about two-thirty. Before breakfast.

"Go ahead." I was laughing already at just the idea of big Newk giving orders to anyone smaller than the Jolly Green Giant.

"It was in the Army. I was three ranks higher than this guy—he was just a Buck—but when I told him he was due for latrine duty, he shook his head. 'Look,' I said, 'it's your *turn.*' He just shook his head again, Jesse. So I walked up to him, stood toe to toe—couldn't stand face to face 'cause his chin came up to about the bottom of my ribs—said, 'That's an *order,* soldier!' Do you know what he said?"

I shook my head, laughing louder.

"He said: 'Have a *white* man tell me. I'm not taking orders from no nigger, no matter how big he is!' "

I tried to keep laughing. After all, that was the punch line. But couldn't. "You know something?" I said.

"What?"

"That's really not so funny at all."

The same kind of expression came over his big face. "You're right."

It's plain what Newk's story actually meant. The other Negro had been so damn brainwashed for so damn long that he really didn't respect another black man, no matter *what* he'd accomplished, no matter how "big" he was. That's the saddest thing that can happen to any race, to any human being.

Maybe some of the extremists *have* taken everything good for their own, maybe they do see everything black as beautiful—even the blackness of some of their own souls. But it could be that this is a necessary first step for a race which almost lost its pride in two centuries of one form or another of slavery. The black man today, the young black man in particular, feels he's doing something important, feels *he's* important. After generations of being told he didn't have what it took to get his family's next meal on the table, how can that be so bad? Of course, I was the rare exception to the tragic rule. My legs not only ran me to world's records and gold medals, but they ran me out of the ghetto so fast and far that, even after a bankruptcy and a federal income tax indictment which took four years to pay off, I'm still living better than most. Even when Ruth and I were first married, teenagers too proud to take anything from our parents (not that they *had* anything) and unable to support ourselves; even when I came home from the Olympics the most famous man in the world and found that the top job available—the only job, really—was Cleveland playground counselor at $1,500 a year; even when the tax thing hit me in 1965 and I found that, with lawyers' fees and all, I was $150,000 in debt with a bank account that had $1,500—it was all only temporary. I knew I'd be putting steak on the table again sometime, just as I knew I'd run out of that Cleveland playground as I'd run out of every other ghetto before it.

I'm not going to lie to you. I *like* living well. It's *good* to live well. I don't have to prove a thing to myself by eating beans and onions or taking cold water showers anymore. I proved *that* in Oakville, Alabama.

But all these years that I'd been working so hard, running so fast away from the torture of the ghetto, I overlooked this: That even though I almost literally had to break my spine (trying to stay the world's fastest human on the golf course with men half my age or simply on an impossible schedule), I *still* was the exception to have even *that* chance. Sure, a paralyzing ruptured spinal disc forced me into surgery in 1965, but too many people in this world don't get the opportunity to break their backs for success. Ruth said it best when we were driving to a civil rights gathering one evening. "By the way," she told me, "we'll be the only couple of color there tonight."

I was a little shocked. Not that Ruth and I hadn't been the only blacks in white circles a number of times in our lives, but *that* night it didn't seem to fit. "What about the Youngs and the Rodners? Or Bob and Sally?" I asked her. "*They* should be there if I am."

She looked at me with tenderness, yet I couldn't help sensing that part of it was the tenderness you feel for a naïve child. "You'll just never quite understand it, will you?"

"What, honey?"

"That the white world will do things for Jesse Owens that it simply will not do—even when it should—for anybody else."

She'd said that to me before. Other people had said it to me. But I hadn't gotten the message, because underneath I'd wanted to think that the world had done things for me it hadn't for anyone else because *I'd* done things no one else had done. Sure, I knew there were more important accomplishments than running and jumping—George Washington Carver did more with a peanut than I could've done in a billion Olympics, one speech of Martin Luther King's might have been worth more than *all* the sports records that exist. But you do your own thing in life, *that* was my thing and, by God, when called, I'd done it the best.

Still, after Ruth said it to me that night a couple of years ago, I found myself thinking about George Washington Carver and Martin Luther King in a different way. What were *their* rewards? Carver never knew a thousandth of the good life that I'd lived. And Martin? Horribly, brutally snuffed out before he was forty.

When we got to the meeting, my white acquaintances were in a good mood. I wasn't.

"Jesse," the president of a large corporation said, coming up to me while eating an expensively prepared hors d'oeuvre. For the first time, I resented it, couldn't touch a spot of their food. "It took me a while, but I just got around to reading your book," he went on. "You exposed those militants the way it needed to be done. Good going."

"I'm afraid I can't accept the compliment," I suddenly heard myself answer. "I'm a militant too."

A shocked look swept over his face. He sputtered, said something about the pennant race, quickly excused himself to go talk to someone else. As the night wore on, I noticed more and more people gathered in little circles buzzing, then suddenly changing the subject when I'd walk up. We left early.

It wasn't that I'd reversed my stand from *Blackthink*. It wasn't that I still didn't know that a hell of a lot of black extremists got money, crude kicks or their own perverted ego trip from militancy, and it certainly wasn't that I believed in setting fire to the buildings where white corporation presidents sat. But I realized now that militancy in the *best* sense of the word was the *only* answer where the black man was concerned, that any black man who wasn't a militant in 1970 was either blind or a coward.

I hadn't given up my idea of an autonomous black middle class. But now I saw that it mainly *was* an idea. In the late 1960's there had seemed to be a real possibility for the average black to become a genuinely middle-class American. He was one or two kinds of people then—an "average" man somewhere between thirty and fifty with a family and a steady job, making less than an average white, still shut out of a lot of things, but with a prospect for higher wages and more doors opening. In other words, he was on the verge of some of the good things in life, the things you can touch *and* the things you can't. I didn't think he was that unhappy with himself and his world, because both of them were getting better.

The other "basic black" was the young one, the son of this man and of the man who hadn't done as well—the hard-core ghetto kid. Yet even *this* boy was being given a chance to go to school, to college. The odds were against him, overwhelmingly against him as far as some things were concerned, but he *did* have a way out. It would take a hell of a lot more elbow grease and grit than it should take, but *he could do it.* More and more like him *were* doing it every year.

I thought.

It hasn't worked out quite that way. Not *enough.* Part of the reason is bigotry, part of the reason is circumstance.

Unlike almost every other Negro, I've voted Republican in most elections. It isn't because I had stashed away somewhere a fortune that I wanted to preserve. I voted Republican, even though it chilled me how Republicans generally restrict our personal freedoms more than the Democrats do, for the same reason all my black friends voted Democratic. Because, until recently, I felt the Republicans had a slightly better chance of saving the country as a result of their economic policies.

In a bankrupt nation, there aren't *any* freedoms.

I've been in personal debt—deep personal debt—several times in my life, and I know how hard it is to get out. For a country, it's next to impossible. Of course, I knew this country had the economic piper to pay before I wrote *Blackthink.* But in the middle sixties, who dreamed that the Vietnam war would go on and on and on, that we'd keep sending men to the moon to collect rocks when millions of our own people, hungry and undereducated, were throwing rocks through windows, that the air we breathe would be almost as corrupt as our politicians?

Nor did I sense how truly committed so many of the young were to something *without* compromises, something neither Democrat *nor* Republican. These are kids who don't want to make a fortune. In a world beset by war, prejudice, pollution, they've come to feel that there's something more important than a license plate with your initials on it. So most of them—the ones who haven't dropped out—are out there making a living, but no more. Their real scene is the key to bigger things than the executive washroom. That means a new kind of America—which is okay by me. The only question is: Who's going to pay for the old one—the America committed to massive programs that would hopefully solve the problems of our old, our poor and, particularly, our disenfranchised black people?

Not that I think all those spend-a-billion programs are the answer anyway. But another depression isn't any answer, either. In the thirties it might have brought people closer, but in the seventies it will split this country in two.

We've got to put on a crash program—not with money, but with *humanity*—to give America back to *all* its people. For this finally isn't just a black problem, it's a *human* problem. Of course, I happen to know the "black" part best. And did *you* know, for example, that the Race Relations Information Center not long ago surveyed the fifty most important corporations in America to see how many black men were executives?

The answer was none.

They went down the line then until they got to the boards of directors, finally finding three. Out of over three thousand.

That's a one to one thousand ratio, a far cry from the ratio of black to white in America. But *more* disturbing is the propaganda written for the white public by white publications whose major advertisers are those same corporations and others like them. Reading the establishment press in America, you'd believe that things are really rosy for Negroes. I remember one article in particular. It appeared in *Parade* a couple of years ago. "A New Trend: Black Bosses for White Workers" it was called. I'll never forget the picture that went with the piece, either. It showed a casually dressed black man seated in a plush chair, looking over the job application of a white who was standing. The white was wearing a tie.

I'm sure the scene actually took place. I'm sure there *are* white men with black bosses. I know some. But I also know that the title of the article—and the impression that it gave—are bullshit.

I make my living mainly through speaking. Some of the time I talk to groups on behalf of some of the biggest corporations in America. Many of the younger generation think I've sold out by doing that. I don't think so. To expect these organizations to pull a black man out of the factory and make him president would be asinine. But one thing would be far worse: To stand by and watch a large corporation *not* try to speed up the day when a Negro *can* be its president—or even President of the United States.

The American League is one of my employers. No major league baseball team has ever had a black manager—as it *should* have, since the majority of the stars are black—but the powers-that-be do allow me to speak freely to them and explain why the sooner it happens, the better. And, because of that, it *will* happen sooner.

To me, this is mainly where it's at: communication between people, not lobbying for this "issue" or that one. "You never talk *issues*," someone accused me recently.

"That's because issues *aren't* the issue," I answered.

Issues are only an outgrowth of the basic problem, sometimes a perversion of it. Open housing, for example, has come to mean "open to Negroes." I don't blame a white man for being angry if someone is arbitrarily ordering his neighbors to cut property values in half by selling to blacks. But the truth is that property values usually go down because other whites have let their ignorance and bigotry run rampant and not because blacks will let the property go to hell. And that very bigotry is at the whole root of the "issue" anyway. Let's be brutally honest: If more blacks than whites *do* let their property go to hell, isn't it because *all* blacks were made to live *in* hell in this country for a hundred and fifty years? Humanity—or inhumanity—is always at the bottom of every "issue."

The proof is that what's true of housing is true of everything else, from drugs to education. What does it matter to a black man named Cliff whether Stokely Carmichael is right in saying whites push drugs into ghetto areas more to deaden revolution than to make a dirty buck, if Cliff has watched the white dope seller ruin *his* twelve-year-old daughter, turned her into a prostitute and then a pusher herself?

Drugs aren't the issue here. The "issue" is why so many millions of black kids are ripe for heroin. The "issue" is how the white peddler-pervert is able to enslave the black youth by charging so much for the heroin that the kid *must* become a whore or an armed robber.

But America is hung up on effects, not causes; "issues," not humanity. We don't see—or do we?—that "issues" are only a cop-out for the big issue of being human, for confronting ourselves. The white dope pusher can enslave and criminalize the black adolescent because a superficial symptom-happy white establishment has repressively outlawed drugs, just as it tries to outlaw every nonviolent "sin" from gambling to sex, creating a black market where a daily pop of H goes for more than any young black can ever make in an honest day's work. And the young black is ripe for that H because a couple of centuries ago some white men outlawed racial equality.

No wonder he becomes a hotblooded militant—if he *can*. Militancy doesn't mean violence—unless violence means survival. Militancy is a lot healthier for the young black than that chillingly cool, apathetic heroin trance. It's a lot healthier for me. And for *you*, whether white or black, young or old, rich or poor.

As a famous younger generation song goes, "A fool plays it cool."

President Richard M. Nixon
Washington, D.C.

Dear Mr. President:

In the 1950's, President Eisenhower and yourself sent me around the globe as Ambassador of Sports for the State Department. My job was to make friends for the United States, and to try to understand what was happening in the rest of the world, then report back to you.

I believed in that, just as I believed in what I did last year when you sent me to the new Ivory Coast in Africa to answer as best I could their questions about America.

There was only one question I couldn't answer during my ten-day stay in the Ivory's capital city of Abidjan. It was asked by an educated teen-age boy over supper in one of their little orphan huts.

"What about Eldridge Cleaver and Angela Davis?" he said to me.

I had no answer for that Abidjanian boy, because suddenly I realized that I had never answered the question for myself. It's one thing to come to an understanding of Cleaver's significance as I have, it's another to come to grips with the significance of why he is in exile from what is supposedly the freest country in the world.

In the days that followed, I gave that boy's question a great deal of thought. On the one hand, I knew that no matter how open I became, no matter how much I changed, I'd never be with Eldridge Cleaver and Angela Davis all the way. But I also saw that it didn't matter.

Eldridge and Angela and those like them must be free—Angela free to walk the streets of her country safely, Eldridge free to fly home from Algiers and not be put in prison. *These* "trips" far outweigh even that of a U. S. President going to Red China (to say nothing of a former runner's going to Ivory Coast).

When analyzing the Cleaver and Davis cases, one inevitably is confronted by the fact that they received special treatment—specially *bad*—because they are more "political criminals" than anything else. What can that mean in America?

I know what it means to a sixteen-year-old Abidjanian boy.

And above and beyond the moral question, though, wouldn't granting a six-month amnesty to Eldridge be a bold, positive political move? Mr. President, if *you* met with these young blacks, listened to them, tried to understand them—and vice versa—the effect might be earthshaking. For *they*, not Chou En-lai, are at the root of the crisis in America today.

But not because they're black. Because they're young, disenfranchised rebels. The more we push these things underground, the more we make for another kind of earthquake.

Mr. President—let my people go.

They're *your* people too. They're the underdog. They're human beings.

Respectfully,
Jesse Owens

In the incongruous country of Algiers, there lives one man who more than any other can take the major step today toward peace between the fissured races—and, more important, between the split generations—in America. Just as in *this* land, long denied the right of bail given to rapists and robbers, is a young woman who also symbolizes those destructive chasms.

To be honest, I don't just disagree with some of what Eldridge and Angela say—I'm a little afraid of them.

But I'm a helluva lot more afraid of living in the kind of country from which men like Eldridge have to flee, and where women like Angela cannot. And I'm more afraid of the polarities and hostilities that arise from these injustices.

Just as the people of this country—*all* the people—must make person-to-person humanity their first priority, so our President must put communication with our expatriates at the very top of his list of priorities. Even the hardest "hard hat" could benefit from such a "Summit Meeting." As a symbol. And as an education—for both the President and the revolutionaries. Today, for example, young blacks themselves—let alone whites—are split over whether the Black Panthers Cleaver created are a defensive, humanistic group or a gang of murderers. I've worked with them, talked *and* listened to them, and I can't give you an exact answer in every case. But I can tell you that they *began* as the first and the longer their heroes and heroines are exiled, the more they'll become the second. At this very moment, the Panther leadership is split, fighting for its life against arrest and incarceration. But the forces that spawned the Panthers are *not* on the run. They exist among all colors and classes, and threaten to murder this nation rather than *be* murdered.

I don't know *what* Eldridge or Angela are guilty of. But I do know that, until convicted of a real crime, they certainly should have been walking the streets of America as free as our syndicate kingpins do. And, if they finally are found guilty of stealing a gun or using one, let the penalty be the same as it would for a WASP corporation president or Mayor Daley.

Don't you see it? Eldridge and Angela—and Jane and Peter Fonda—are the *new* "corporation" in this country, a corporation of *ideas,* and if we can do business with Red China, why can't we do the business of communicating with this new generation that believes in its country enough to stay, to risk constant abuse and even imprisonment?

A lot of rhetoric?

Let me tell it to you on the level *I* really understand. I realize that the athletic field seems a far cry from the solemn arenas of morality and politics, but underneath them all there's an important connection.

In 1948, Mel Patton beat my 1936 mark of 9.4 seconds for the hundred-yard dash—by a tenth of a second. It took almost another twelve years for the next tenth to be chipped off. And whenever I appeared at colleges or athletic competitions, one of the questions I'd almost *always* be asked—after the four-minute mile started to be run—was, "Jesse, do you think they'll ever run the hundred in nine flat?" Finally, *Ebony* magazine came and asked me to write a piece on it. I was never more sure of anything than I was of what I said in that article. "They'll Never Run the Miracle Hundred!" was its title. I marshaled every argument in the book—and some no one had ever heard of—to make my case.

I told the world about the limits of the human body's consumption of oxygen. About how evolution has constructed man's lungs to do only so much before he simply passes out.

I told them about an athelete's "instinct," how when I'd run the 9.4 hundred in the thirties, I'd sensed inside myself that I couldn't have pushed my body one speck harder. I granted that better shoes and track surfaces and a good tail wind and improved training methods and a dozen other things could all add up to a 9.3 hundred, maybe even 9.2.

I told them about the four-minute mile being kid stuff next to the nine-flat hundred, how the sub-four-minute mile was really an endurance achievement, not a *speed* achievement. Running a mile under four minutes was actually a test of how long the physical/physiological mechanism can keep up a fine but not at all impossible speed. Going a hundred yards in nine seconds flat would, on the other hand, be an actual breakthrough of human potential. The human animal could cover twenty-two plus feet a second (which is what a four-minute mile amounts to) for longer and longer periods, until he finally went twenty-three feet a second, even twenty-five. But he'd never do more than thirty-three feet a second, which is what a nine-flat hundred would require. You'd need a true superman for *that.*

History bore me out too. Good old history. I told them how in thirty-five years the record for the mile had been lowered more than fifteen seconds (and it would have been more if Paavo Nurmi hadn't been ahead of his time and run a 410.4 in 1923). The hundred-yard sprint, on the other hand, had been done in 9.8 by B. D. Darbyshire in 1864! In a century, we had improved barely half a second.

I told them about the sprinters on the scene, how each had one or two characteristics that could make for a "miracle hundred," but that none of them could possibly have it all put together anatomically because that would mean a mixture of opposites. The ideal "superman" would have to have the power of a prime football fullback with the lightning speed of a cheetah. He'd have to have the getaway reflexes of a Jesse Owens and the thunderclap finish of a Ralph Metcalfe. His legs would have to be out of proportion to the rest of his body, longer, which would probably mean that he'd be a Negro, yet he'd have to have been taught by a top white coach since he was five years old—because no black track coaches had ever been allowed to reach the highest echelon in their field. He'd have to have the ability to relax thoroughly at the crucial moment, yet be supremely ambitious and intense for that extra "nth" of motivation, to say nothing of the years of training three hours a day six days a week. He'd have to have been free of serious pneumonia or respiratory troubles, yet made metal-strong in that one incomparable way: being exposed to the elements.

Even with all that, the best I gave him was 9.1.

And I've been right—but *wrong*. That's why I risked boring you with every last detail. Because it doesn't matter if you've got a million arguments, doesn't matter if your ideas are still "working"—if the reason you believe them is because, underneath it all, you don't *want* anyone to run the hundred in nine flat. I was like the man who fell off the top floor of a thirty-five story building, yelling happily, "I'm all right so faaaaarrrr. . . ."

"So far" isn't good enough, I've learned.

I have changed where the nine-flat hundred is concerned, where some of my most basic attitudes are concerned. If I hadn't, I think I would've hit bottom in a way much more significant and permanent than a bankruptcy or a double pneumonia.

I want this country to change course before it hits bottom.

I've said this so often I sound like a broken record, but I'll say it again: There are an awful lot of good things, great things, unique things about America. But how much can they mean, how long can they last, if an Eldridge Cleaver or an Allison Krause can't be a part of them?

If personal honesty is the issue in life, just as it is in this book—and it *is*—if where it's really at is digging down through all the dirty laundry of your soul and finding the truth, then nothing can be more important to the truth of a country than an example set by those in symbolic power. I believe that the single most significant act the President of the United States could make today to heal the hemorrhaging wound of America would be to grant Eldridge Cleaver six months' amnesty to come home and talk—and listen—to his Panthers, talk to middle-class blacks, liberal whites, and to the President himself.

When the embittered Cleaver was unexpectedly released from jail a few years ago, he couldn't hold back his tears. "I don't *believe* it!" he sobbed. Let him—and so many others—say it again now. Let them have tears in their eyes—rather than hate in their hearts—for justice in this nation.

After Eldridge exiled himself in Algiers, a "Kilroy" line swept America. I still see it written on a public bathroom now and then. "Eldridge Cleaver," it says. "Please call your office."

It isn't funny.

It's the blackest of black humor.

For that line isn't really a joke. It's a ruptured nation's unconscious but final poignant plea for the communication between human beings which alone can heal.

We must allow the Eldridge Cleavers of this country to call their offices once again. If we don't, let's have no wide-eyed handwringing when all the phones go dead.

Of course, I could be wrong. Maybe I'm overreacting to make up for the time I didn't react enough. Maybe I've begun to glimpse the finish line ahead of *me* and suddenly feel a sense of urgency I never did before. Maybe this is just the other side of the coin of the "impossible" nine-flat hundred.

Maybe.

But one thing I know for sure.

Somewhere in Abidjan, a teen-age boy thinks that the United States of America is full of shit.

. . . BUT SOME THINGS NEVER CHANGE

Missy
Traveling in a Trailer Somewhere
in America

Dear Missy,

Several winters ago, you wrote me a letter asking what color Christmas was.

You said you'd asked a lot of people, including your parents and older brothers and sisters, and that most of them had laughed at you and none had really listened to you or answered your question.

You were only in grammar school—when you *went* to school—and didn't even have a place where I could write back because you and your parents and five kin lived in a trailer. And because you never told me your last name.

By now you're probably in high school, and I wonder if your question has been answered yet. Frankly, I wonder if the world has taught you to laugh at and finally forget your own unique, pure wisdom.

I hope not. Because the more I thought about it, the more I realized you'd asked the most important question anyone can.

I didn't have the answer then, Missy. Now—now I think I might.

Your friend,
Jesse Owens

It's a cliché that youth is our real hope. But it becomes more than mere cliché when we add that youth can *only* save us if we endeavor to save *them.*

To a great degree, we have not saved ourselves. We were young once, and we—as a nation and, too often, as individuals—have lost not only youth but lost the spirit of youth, too. If we had been willing to stand the pain of seeing how rigid we were growing with the years, we would have retained the pliability of character that asks questions like, "What color is Christmas?"

Missy's letter to me was a long one, as nine-year-olds' letters go. She went into three scrawling pages about why she was confused. Missy had heard a prominent black leader say that Negroes should celebrate a "black Christmas." The song everyone sang in December, however, spoke of a "white Christmas." Yet to her, Christmas was green, like the colors of the trees she'd always had in her home, and red, like Santa Claus's suit, and maybe a little silver like the wrapping on the one present her parents scraped to buy her each year.

It's true that Jesse Jackson and other leading blacks have called for a "black Christmas," just as they've called for black Easters and black everything elses. It may make good copy in the newspapers, but it doesn't make such good copy inside formative minds. For Christmas should only be exactly what it is to Missy.

Even though I held down three jobs to go to college in the thirties and felt lucky merely to sit in the *classes,* let alone "sit-in" anywhere else, I'm still mostly on the side of today's students. Mainly, it's because I do feel a world where you reach manhood only to be sent off to risk losing your life in a ludicrous war or, if you're lucky, stay home and slowly die of pollution or poverty *is* a world built on some pretty rotten hypocrisies.

But the color of Christmas transcends all that. I really believe it. I've *seen* it, seen it in the homes of thousands of ghetto kids. Just as I saw it in my own ghetto home fifty years ago.

The horror of Cleveland will always be one of my nightmares.

My father moved the ten of us up there from Alabama because he and my mother were convinced that nothing could be worse than the sharecropping existence. Cleveland did give me a new life, was a little better for my brothers and sisters and even my mother. But not for my father. Being a black man in Cleveland in the "Golden Twenties" was worse than everything he had ever known. And he'd known a lot. My mother and sisters cleaned the houses of whites and took in laundry, my brothers—all older—found three or four hours a day of heavy crate loading or manure shoveling. Even I was able to shine shoes, tend a greenhouse and get a few hours filling gas tanks.

Yet Henry Owens never found steady work in all the years we lived up north. Finally, when I broke world's records in my last year of high school and was offered scholarships (and usually a lot more) to half the colleges in the country, I was able to trade all that for working my way through Ohio State on the one condition that the state find a permanent position for Henry Owens.

There was one other condition, too—that this proud man never know how he got the job. In my mind that wasn't deception or charity. I knew he'd work harder at it than anyone else they could get. And he did, till the day he died shortly after my mother at the beginning of the Second World War.

But those fifteen years before I went to college—they were rough ones for Henry Owens. The first ten or so were cruel because we never had enough to eat, holes in everything we wore, and he took it as *his* fault. When things began to get better for us, when I became a "celebrity" and my brothers and sisters graduated to better jobs (our poverty never allowed most of them to graduate from school), it was worse in a way. Happy as my father was for us, he felt useless, felt he'd failed. More than once he trudged home at night after being turned down or laid off from still another half-time quarter-pay job and dragged an old wicker chair over in the corner, sat kind of almost facing the wall. We all knew to let him be, but you couldn't help seeing his shoulders spasm every few minutes as he fought back the tears for maybe the ten-thousandth time.

After a while, a long while sometimes, he'd get up and reach for the family Bible, take it back to the chair, turning a little toward the room. Then he'd sit fingering through it, stopping at a page here or there, looking hard at the words. He couldn't read them. But it gave him strength all the same.

Just as *he* gave *us* strength each Christmas—enough strength, enough of a glimpse of what *could* be, to last the whole rest of the year.

First, we had meat for dinner, no matter what. Oh, how I treasured that feast. Of course, we didn't have our Christmas dinner on Christmas Eve like the whites in Cleveland did.

We ate it the night after. Because that was when we had our tree.

Henry Owens didn't have the money to buy a tree. But he always was able to go out Christmas Day and find heavy work hauling away the unsold ones. Part of his pay was one of those trees. As the sun went down, he carried it home on his back and, the instant he walked in the door, we'd all grab it from him excitedly and set it up in the big room.

We decorated it with anything we had. There were no ornaments on our tree. Every year my mother hung her three pieces of jewelry on the branches, my brothers and sisters and I put some of our tattered pieces of clothing on it. We gave no gifts. And we didn't expect our hole-riddled stockings to be filled with anything. It was a blessing just to have our socks hanging there from that Christmas tree!

I'll have to admit it was a motley looking thing. But without that tree, I never would've had the spirit inside to somehow get to the Olympics and take home the four little symbolic trees they gave me with my four gold medals.

What I'm saying is that I couldn't have survived psychologically without that tree. Each December 26, it told me that no matter *what* you had to go through to get there, Christmas was waiting at the end of the struggle.

As I said, I realize fully that the life experiences of today's black ghetto or even white suburb young aren't at all the same as they were for an emaciated kid named James Cleveland Owens in the twenties.

Still, I wonder if that doesn't mean that *they* need some kind of Christmas even more. I wonder if moving away from *that* kind of Christmas isn't moving away from tomorrow rather than yesterday. Possibly with a few things like that "old-fashioned" Christmas in our homes today, there wouldn't be as much alcohol or drugs or violence or bitter generation gaps.

Christmas isn't religion, you see. You don't even have to believe in God to celebrate it. Christmas isn't "establishment." You can celebrate it any darned way you like—even a day late and without tinsel.

Christmas *is* celebration. Even when you thought there was nothing to celebrate.

Christmas is the *future*—a future when skin color and all the other artificial differences between men mean nothing.

Christmas is *peace on earth.* For a little while anyway.

Missy, I think you asked the best question I've ever heard in almost sixty years of living on this earth.

For you were so right. Christmas isn't white, unless it snows.

And it isn't black, except for those who've never known it.

Color it green and red, honey—with a dash of silver wrapping.

Prime Minister Houphoët-Boigny
Abidjan, Ivory Coast,
Africa

Dear Mr. Houphouët-Boigny:

Most people in this world think of the new as change. But sometimes the new on the grandest political scale ends up affirming the most simple, enduring human values. If only two hundred million Americans could somehow spend a few days in your "new" country as I did, I know they would be renewed as I was with the capacity for hope and hard work which never seems to die, no matter how oppressed or poor the people.

Jesse Owens

Abidjan is a relaxed but industrious little town in a beautiful little country about the area of Arizona with about as much population as Chicago. That population is composed of many faiths: Moslems, Catholics, Protestants, animists. Though surrounded by imposing nations like Ghana and Liberia, Ivory Coast has in only a handful of years developed an economy greater than any other West African country. As in Israel, the black people there are working together and hard for something in which they believe.

And the government is allowing them to do it, is really but a mirror-reflection of the people's needs and desires. Their prime minister is an open, good man who believes in dialogue to solve problems—dialogue based upon some very simple, very old principles.

One outcome of those dialogues, of those principles, is how the Ivory Coast orphans have been given "homes"—when no homes, almost no physical shelter or food, seemed possible for them. Being new and, most important, being made up of the homeless and disenfranchised from all other parts of Africa, Ivory Coast suddenly found itself with thousands upon thousands of starving youngsters—from teen-agers to infants—who had no parents, no known relatives. Some were taken in by the least poor Ivory Coast families. A few were taken into the home of Félix Houphouët-Boigny himself.

But these were only stopgap measures. Something had to be done for future homeless who would be too young or too weak to work. So Abidjan began a kind of unique "Boys' Town," where huts were set up in which the older youngsters took care of the younger! To my knowledge, there's nothing quite like it on this earth.

The huts in which the orphans live, however, could not be completely built and kept up by ten- or even sixteen-year-olds, especially when they have to be father and mother to so many other eight-, five- and one-year-olds there. The United States heard and helped. We not only saved several old huts, but built much-needed new ones, plus giving an entire library and paving their main street for them. Though there are countless—and I *mean* countless—black men and women in America more deserving than yours truly, President Nixon donated the library in the name of Jesse Owens, and the Ivory Coast celebrated my coming by naming that main street de la Rue Jesse Owens. Once I began to know the people who walked along that street, I felt as proud as I ever had in my life. The Abidjanians still have poverty, but almost no crime —though the young, even those who come out of the huts, are very Western and very rebellious just like our own. Yet it's a disagreement without disrespect. It was a real lesson to me that such an attitude could pervade a whole country.

I was there for only ten days, but what I learned—not in "rules" I can give or insights I can even name —made it seem like a year. At the same time, as I look back, it seemed like my stay in Ivory Coast was only hours, as is the way with those rare times in one's life that are pure joy.

There was the opening of the main street, not because it was a tribute to me, but because it was a tribute to understanding between peoples. There were forty-eight different foreign nations represented at that ceremony. And the warmth between us wasn't plastic, because we were all touched by this feeling that pervaded the Abidjanians. And I think we all went back to our vastly different homes resolved to impart that to our own peoples.

There was the athletic competition, with the young Ivory Coast boys and girls competing against Ghana. They felt no bitterness when they lost, no pompousness when they won. They were glad just to be in the arena, to be a part of the world. In the deepest sense, they were glad to be alive. I kept thinking of what Martin once said to me shortly after one of his greatest personal defeats. "Well, Jesse," he smiled, "I guess a lot of people didn't even wake up this morning."

But most of all, there were the informal talks with the youngsters. I had fruitful discussions with the ministers from foreign nations, spoke at length to the heads of state of Ivory Coast, met with parents, was in frequent touch with our own Secretary of State Rogers—but the most memorable moments were the quiet conversations with the young, and sometimes the silences, proving to me once again, as youth all over the world has for decades now, that the communication gap can always be bridged by an open mind and a good heart.

Youth has the truth.

Dear Rich—

Wherever you are, I'm sure you're productive and reasonably happy.

Because *you* changed, and that was one of the most important proofs in my life that some things never do change—and never should.

J. O.

The sixteen-year-old brown face was laced white with long, open cuts.

"*Why*, Rich?" I implored him.

"It's our territory," he whispered. "They don't *belong* here."

"Their parents moved here for a better life," I said. "Like *yours* did. How in the hell can you hold that against them?"

"It's all *we* got. It's our *territory*. We warned 'em." He paused for a second as the pain from a raw cut ate into him. "We'll kill them, every one of 'em, if they stay."

"*You* were almost the one who was killed this time, Rich!"

He shook his head. "Doesn't matter. It's *ours*. It's all we got, J.O.!"

I tried to reach him. "It's all you've got *now*, boy," I said. "But there's more. I promise you, there's more."

He stared in my eyes, bitter, defiant. But I thought I saw just a trace of hope there, too. "*What?*"

The place was the Ida B. Wells Housing Development in Chicago, the year was 1958. And the problems—they were bad, bone bad. Youth can go wrong, too.

But they were solvable problems. And they weren't *that* different from the problems of today.

Four hundred kids were feuding—life-and-death-feuding—in two highly organized, warring camps of hate. Twice now, the leader of one, "Richard III," as he called himself (because he secretly read a little Shakespeare now and then), had been a quarter of an inch from death. First, it was a homemade bomb. This time it had been from a knife wound in his back. The slashes on his face were only window dressing.

Rich had gotten out of the hospital in two days where it would've taken most kids two weeks. Part of it was that Chicago never did too well by black "juvenile delinquent" charity cases. But most of it was that he had a hundred and ninety "troops" to lead. He was going to lead them that night.

Rich was violent but he knew Shakespeare. Rich was violent because that was the *only* way he knew how to survive in the jungle he'd been raised in. I was trying to teach him another way.

It was five in the afternoon when we had that talk. The rumble was to go off at ten that night. Yes, the words have changed. It isn't "rumble" anymore. Or "juvenile delinquent." And Rich was a "Negro" then, not a "black." But I've seen it all and let me tell you that the names are just about the only thing that has changed.

I was working part-time for the state of Illinois trying to control juvenile delinquency through sports. After a week on the job, I realized there'd be a lot more to it than tossing a basketball around. Fortunately, to Rich and the several hundred others like him there I wasn't the fuzz or establishment or anything like that. Though I was in my forties—an age most of them never expected to get anywhere near—I was a hero of sorts, not because of my gold medals, but because I'd come out of a sharecropper ghetto that even they respected and had gotten the world to call me "mister" without losing my roots.

It had taken a month to get into their confidence, another month to be allowed in their headquarters. And I don't know how long it took after that to actually exchange ideas with them. Except that, where ideas were concerned, they felt it was more blessed to give than receive. And I knew that if they went through with this rumble to end all rumbles, *that* would prove to *them* once and for all *life* was a jungle.

Ida B. Wells Development at the time was a fishbowl for the entire city. Sure, there was violence all over, and it wouldn't turn off automatically no matter what happened with Rich and his gang, and Juan and his. But it could change the direction.

I didn't tell them not to have the rumble. I didn't *tell* them anything. There was far too much bitterness in those boys to ask them flat out to consider *never* venting it. What I did do was try somehow to temporarily channel all that hate, not dam it.

"Postpone the rumble for one night," I said. "Till I can prove something to you."

Reluctantly, they agreed—only because they knew *I'd* cool it, not tell a soul, difficult as it would be for me, if they chose to go ahead instead. Rich and Juan met and set it for the same time the following night at the I. C. train tracks. But they didn't see what difference a day would make.

That next day was a Saturday. They didn't have any school, those of them who would've gone anyway. "My" half of the deal was that Rich and Juan—and six guys from each of their sides—would spend that day with me. I was gambling that by dusk I would have given them the breath of something else in life worth as much as a meaningless plot of land in front of a housing development.

The Saturday night rumble didn't come off. That night or any other. I'm not telling you I was able to change everything for the better in twenty-four hours. Far from it. There'd be individual knife fights that night, and a lot of nights afterward. There'd still be bitterness and hate. And wasted lives.

But less. Less. Because I *was* able to show Rich and Juan and a dozen of their "brothers" a world they'd never seen. Oh, they'd seen it with their eyes, yet never with their emotions, because it had always been from the outside in. For once I'd put them on the *inside* looking out.

They loved cars, these kids. So I'd taken them downtown to a parking lot where all the hikers were black. The owner was white, but a friend. He let Rich and a few of the others park some cars. I bought them a good lunch. Then we went back, parked a few more cars, rode the employees' wild escalating ladder from the underground to the top level.

Then Sid offered Rich and Juan jobs.

Four days a week after school and all day Saturdays and Sundays. Rich and Juan were to park those groovy cars. They'd be paid a fair wage for it, too. Juan would start in two weeks. Rich would start in one hour.

He'd have a *real* job.

Work he was *good* at.

Money in his *pocket.*

Self-respect.

How *could* the rumble come off that Saturday night? You couldn't have a rumble when the leader of the aggressor gang was parking cars in a downtown Chicago garage. "We still gotta settle with those cats some way," he growled at me in front of his chief lieutenants.

"We'll talk about it," I said.

We never talked about it. It was already settled, though Rich didn't know it.

His example settled things for 90 percent of those around him. And for kids eight, ten, twelve, who weren't in the gangs yet, who watched the example of Rich and all those who followed in his footsteps one way or another. Some came to me, asked what kind of jobs *they* could get. Others couldn't bring themselves to go that far. But at least they were a half a step farther away from knife fights and uncontrollable bitterness.

Naturally it didn't always work out even for those who got a job or hit the books. But more often than not it did, and more often than not then they went on to better jobs, some even to college.

Not that it was any cinch. Rich started work at four that crucial afternoon. At a quarter to six I was dressing to catch a plane to London when the phone rang. It was the owner of the garage.

"Jesse—this kid you hired," he began.

"What's up?"

"He banged a fender. It happens. I'm willing to go along. But *he* wants to quit. I know how much this means to you so I called."

"Put him on, Sid."

I missed my plane, but convinced Rich to stay, caught a later flight.

I returned home four days later, made two calls from the airport, one to Ruth, the second to the garage. Rich wasn't there.

I threw on slacks and a tee shirt, drove down to Ida Wells. In a typical apartment where the dishwashers were used as garbage cans and the elevators as urinals, I found his younger brother. Rich was in jail.

I hurried to the police station. They said he'd stolen an auto. I knew Rich might put a knife in another fellow who'd threatened "*his* territory," but he'd never take something that *wasn't* his. A strange code? Not if you've been there.

"I didn't do it, J.O.," he told me, but with the old bitterness surging back. "These two guys offer me a ride home—they weren't even from Ida. I say sure. All of a sudden some sirens start and they pull over to the side and split. The car's stolen."

Every life has its turning point. For me it was when father left the prison security of the sharecropping South for Cleveland. For Rich it was when he was put in jail for something he didn't do after he'd done all he could to change from gang leader to solid citizen.

Almost.

I talked to the police two and a half hours. I talked to the Commissioner. I got the Governor on the phone. I began at a quarter to one on a Thursday afternoon. At 11:20 that night, they let Rich walk out of jail. I knew him for six years after that and he never went back in. I'd almost bet my life he hasn't ever been in again.

I don't tell the story to glorify myself. Rich helped me as much as "J.O." helped him. I tell it because the gangs of yesterday aren't altogether different from the gangs of today. No, 1972's "juvenile delinquents" usually don't want jobs in parking lots. In fact, *I* first coined the phrase "the new Mafia" to describe teen-age terrorists, both black and white, who make life intolerable for average- middle- and lower-class Americans today the way the Riches and Juans never did. I was one of the first to ask whether that new Mafia will spread beyond the ghettos, beyond the cities themselves.

But the increasing threat of violence from the gangs today is not as much because the young have changed as because *we* haven't. The gap has grown, when it should have narrowed.

Just before I wrote this chapter, for instance, I was invited to help form and advise an interracial citizen's committee in the East to deal with gang violence. At the beginning of the meeting, the chairman started distributing some mimeographed sheets containing a list of "teen words" and their definitions. After twenty minutes, the "discussions" hadn't gone any farther than talking about the list!

I politely said I thought we could spend the time to better advantage.

"If you don't know their language, you can't rap with them," some hair-rinsed socialite in a fur coat too hot for the room answered.

"That's true," I said, "But it's *what* they're communicating to us that we've got to understand."

The meeting improved. About a half a percent.

"They don't seem to like us *playing the dozens.*"

"Once they get their *noses open* then we can *stone* the violence."

"I think we ought to concentrate on influencing the *crumbcrushers.*"

And so on.

It was really laughable—except that the situation

was too serious to laugh at. While they were sitting on their behinds using hip words, the afternoon edition of the newspaper would be preparing a story on two teens beating an entire family to death—reason unknown. Who cared whether you called grammar schoolers crumbcrushers? The point was to know what made some of them into skullcrushers.

What was true of this "progressive" group is true of most action groups today, whether the problem is teen violence or job bigotry. You can only pierce the problem on one level—the *human* one. *That* hasn't changed. Any *other* way you go about trying to make things better which operates at the expense of the human level is doomed to make things worse.

Kids—like adults—want self-esteem. The ways you can help them achieve it may be far different now than in 1958, but what human beings, fourteen or fifty-nine years old, want to achieve, *have* to achieve to survive psychologically is always the same.

Yet what about the ones who *want* trouble, who *want* violence, who *want* to bring everything down around them just for the sake of seeing it fall? What do you do about *them?* Fundamentally, *that* hasn't changed either.

Last year, I visited a small Negro parish in Tennessee. I talked to the young minister and he told me about a "joke" that had been played on him—and had taught him more about the bad ones than he'd ever learned in all his twenty-eight years put together.

There had been three gangs in his town, at war with each other but also at war with anybody who walked the streets after the sun started to go down. Crime after crime had been committed—far out of proportion to the population—and the local officials were getting ready to ask for help from the National Guard. Things were really bad.

Beneath all the layers, the trouble could be traced to one nineteen-year-old kid. He was a real bad one. He ruled his gang with an iron hand, but would sacrifice anybody close to him—once it had been one of his own brothers—just to gain a little more power. After two years, *everyone* was his enemy, and *four* unsuccessful attempts had been made on his life in the last month. The fourth had left him blind in one eye. Gil knew it was get out of town for good or get killed. And soon.

So he beat them all to the punch. Gil held his own funeral.

He staged his killing—just like in the movies—with the faked blood, fake police in the uniforms, everything. At his "funeral," he was decked out in Sunday best, cleverly fixed with a pad on his chest and special makeup on his face so that you couldn't actually tell that he was breathing.

One by one, the members of the gangs passed by the open coffin to pay their last respects. Little did they know that that night Gil planned to be in another part of the country with everything in the treasury, as well as anything he could hock that they'd ever stolen.

The second-in-command from one of the other gangs stopped at the casket. "You son-of-a-bitch," he said to the "dead" man. Then softer, "But I feel a little sorry for you. A *little*."

Another hood sauntered up. "Too bad," he said. "But you deserved it."

"I hated your damn guts," the leader of one of the rival camps said between his teeth as he passed by, "but I guess I'll get it the same way, too. So, so long, you poor bastard."

Finally, after just about everyone had filed out, a well-dressed figure came up to where the corpse lay. It was Gil's only remaining brother, and he didn't walk, he limped, because Gil had broken both his legs in a fight when they were younger. He spoke so low the reverend could hardly hear.

"You bastard," he whispered. "You made me a cripple, and what have I got for it? I'm not even the new leader. It's not enough that you're dead, Gil. Not enough! I'm only sorry that *they* killed you. *I* wanted to do it. Well, maybe *this* is the best I can get, but at least it's something!"

With that, he brought out a foot-long knife and held it above his brother.

Gil opened both his eyes. "I'll make *you* the leader, Dave!" he whispered loudly and frantically. "I promise! I'll make you the leader!"

Yes, there are the bad ones. But they can be reached, too.

All Violent Revolutionaries
United States of America

To Whom It May Concern:

Ever hear of New Zealand's Polynesian/White crisis?

Of course you haven't. One reason is that, living in America, we tend to think of our own race problems as the only ones in the world. Or, at the very least, that what happens here means everything to the rest of the world.

It isn't true. We may be the most powerful country around, but more often than not we're a dumb giant, actually following someone else's lead instead of setting our own style. And that goes double for you who've been brainwashed to believe that nothing can *really* change in this country unless you first smash it into little pieces.

Well, the real reason you doom-lovers haven't heard about New Zealand's Polynesian/White crisis is because there isn't one—anymore. And how it was solved might blow your minds, as well as tell the rest of the public, a public which has gotten too damned used to hearing sirens or picking up newspapers with violent headlines, something important, something we seemed to know once but have forgotten.

Jesse Owens

I first became acquainted with New Zealand in the mid-1950's when I was International Ambassador of Sports for President Eisenhower. New Zealand had a problem with its races then—a huge problem. That's one of the reasons I went there. When I returned a couple of years ago, I was shocked by the amazing improvement that had been made between the *Maori* (yellows) and the *Pakeha* (whites).

First, integration had taken place on every level. Polynesians were in Congress, women as well as men. Yellow and white kids were going to school together without bussing or anything resembling it. Intermarriage was taking place without one bit of fuss—most people were proud to have grandchildren of mixed races, in fact! What it all added up to was that an overwhelming majority of New Zealanders had gotten to the point where they thought human-to-human, not color-to-color.

No, I'm not simplistic enough to suggest that a couple of islands the size of Alabama and New York could be any kind of a neat analogy for a melting pot place like the U.S. Yet in one important sense, there had been an even more fulminant situation on those two little islands—with the *Maori,* who were the original New Zealanders until the *Pakeha* came in and took over, owning more bitterness than the American Indian and greater numbers than the American Negro. Like America, New Zealand had been colonized by the British, but it too became a melting pot for everyone from Danes to Chinese to Greeks. Many eastern Europeans in particular have emigrated there since the Second World War.

So how was New Zealand able to "overcome" when we're hearing more and more in America that bitterness is inevitable and mass violence a legacy we cannot escape? Within the history of this small country there is a key lesson not just for Americans of different races, but for Americans of different thinking on *any* significant issue.

For violent revolutionaries, it is this: *The worth of a cause finally can be measured only by the happiness it gives its people during THEIR lives.* To put it plain: If everyone has to sacrifice everything, who's the winner? Those vague, unborn future generations? That's the party line of every totalitarian all the way back to the pathetically oppressed Egyptian pyramid-builders who dropped from the huge stones they carried like flies so that some accidental aristocrat could please his primitive gods.

I'll never forget my conversation with one twenty-three-year-old black revolutionary in New York several years ago. I'd known him before he was into revolution. He'd been in real bad psychological trouble, then suddenly had met a girl, fallen in love, and changed overnight.

A white girl.

One of his problems had been impotency—contrary to the myth of the supersexual black male. Now all that was different, and good. As good as it could be. He and his sweetheart lived together, went everywhere together—even to black revolution raps. At first, she'd been grudgingly accepted by most of them, but, as the extremists within the movement got more intransigent, he began to lose his standing because he was in love with a white woman. One of the leaders—a name you'd know—took him aside one day, told him, "You'll have to choose between your blackness or your white whore."

Jana had given Roger more than just his physical manhood back. She'd given him Manhood with a capital M. Affection—which he'd never had in his "home" (and which probably was what robbed him of his masculinity to begin with). Simple good times. *Real* purpose. Now he was being told he'd have to give all that up for the pseudo-respect of some pseudo-intellectuals who wanted desperately to believe that anything that wasn't black couldn't be beautiful, that a white face or two in a demonstration or at a genuine liberation meeting would ruin the color scheme.

I said it to him as I've said it so many times to so many people: Black isn't beautiful, white isn't beautiful. Handsome is as handsome *does.* Jana was as much into the liberation of human beings as anyone I'd ever met, knowing in her heart that freedom is color-blind. That's why she was able to fall totally in love with Roger.

But Roger wouldn't accept the message of his soul —though "soul" ironically was an unwritten password among his "brothers." "I'll have to give her up," he said to me, his voice quaking.

"For what, Rog? For *what?*" I kept asking him.

A few months after they broke up I was in New York again, bumped into one of his "brothers" in an elevator. We stopped on the street to argue it for a minute.

"He's going to make a lot of lives better, man!" the revolutionary finally snapped at me.

"Maybe," I said. "But one thing's for sure."

"What's that?"

"He's already ruined two."

The oppressed *Maori* in New Zealand didn't want to be martyrs. A lot of them even had to leave the country temporarily to do it—but they carved out an education for themselves, learned a trade, took over part of City Hall instead of bombing it.

And the *Pakeha?*

There we have a lesson for American white liberals who want to change everything except their own *status quo*. The *Pakeha* didn't shudder when the *Maori* began returning or turning up as educated and capable as *they* were. No, the *Maori* were welcomed, respected. Integration into all strata of society was a natural step after that, as inevitable as too many think violence is.

Today in America there may not be a third moral position between militant and moderate, but there *is* a third alternative to the plastic conservative and liberal tags which are constantly being thrown at us. For, in the race crisis or any other crisis, there is another way besides passive isolation or violent activism. And that the circle goes so much wider than race is part of what it's all about. We've come down too hard on the "race problem" in this country, letting the more fundamental *communication* problem get away.

I call that problem "gapthink." Like "blackthink," gapthink is the accepting—sometimes the deliberate making—of unnecessary boundaries in our relationships, of false fences between people, of crucial chasms which communication can't bridge.

Not that every communication chasm can be bridged, or each bridge crossed. But we'd better try. Because if you *believe* that human beings can live together, understand each other, it makes all the difference. The instant Lutz Long, Hitler's prize broad-jumper, threw his arm around me at the crucial moment after I'd failed again and was only one bad jump away from being entirely eliminated from the all-important broad jump, when he asked me what was wrong and really meant it—even though it was in broken English with a German accent thicker than a shotputter's bicep—he bridged the language gap, the race gap, the "enemy" gap completely and forever.

What I felt in that moment before Lutz reached out to me, reached inside me, is perhaps the blindness that produces gapthink more than other. A fearful bitterness—a bitter fear that beneath it all the world is against us. This isolates us from others, makes us feel that the hands reaching out to us are really threatening us.

In one sense, Berlin had been that for me—since I'd arrived. For the first time, I was thousands of miles and an ocean from my wife and family. I wanted to communicate with my own teammates, but it was hard. I'd been given too much publicity. Too much was expected of me. How could I let them know I was scared? As for Hitler and his cronies, they definitely hated me, and it was only natural to wonder if all his athletes also didn't, and the Germans in the huge packed stadium. And the German referee who said I'd fouled on my jump.

In one split second Lutz changed all that for me. At his own expense, too, because with his advice I qualified and went on to win, setting a new record which surpassed the record *he'd* set the jump before. Yet when I won, he raced over and threw that same arm around my shoulder once more.

"Don't you care? Don't you *really* care?" I asked him later when we were together drinking coffee in the Olympic Village.

"I am here to struggle to win, Jesse," he answered in that now-familiar broken English. "But the first one I wish to beat is always *myself*."

I feel the New Zealanders—though they're still human with a lot of faults—have won an important triumph over themselves. So possibly it's not just the size of New Zealand or any accident of fate that they were the first people to give women the vote, or to give everyone—*everyone*—the opportunity to pick up the phone and actually talk to the Prime Minister.

And just as gapthink widens and deepens when given into, so it runs like a ghetto roach when you meet it and fight it. Communication multiplies communication. Humanity begets humanity. Because of what it has accomplished, New Zealand's pride in itself has grown. Its people consider themselves innovators and have almost a hunger to make even bigger strides in all areas of human relations.

I honestly believe that in America we've lost our pride. Communication is at an all-time dangerous low. Whites feel guilty about blacks, blacks are bitter toward whites. Parents are resentful against kids, kids mistrustful of anyone over thirty. Women against men. Homosexuals against straights. Consumers against manufacturers and on and on and on. Yes, much of it *is* an inevitable legacy from past mistakes and, yes, much of the same thing is taking place in other spots on the globe. But only in this ironic incredible mass-communications center which is America do we have so much talk about all of it and so little real *communicating*. We have become a top-heavy nation of "experts" in human relations with hardly anyone possessing a single ounce of groundwork know-how.

When I was in New Zealand recently, I exchanged thoughts and experiences with a lot of working people. One happened to be an electrician who just the week before had fixed a wire in the Prime Minister's place. "It only took me twenty minutes," the man told me. "But I charged him thirty dollars."

"That's pretty steep," I said.

"That's what the Prime Minister thought," the man

smiled. "He told me, 'I'd like this bill itemized, Art. We don't have money to waste in this country.' Of course, when I first got there, there wasn't a light working. He had candles burning! I'd seen wiring like that one time before and found the bad one faster than you can tie your shoe. Everything went right on again. But he wondered if because I was in and out so fast the price to the government shouldn't have been lower, you know?"

"How *did* you itemize it?"

"FOR NEW PIECE OF WIRE: ½ DOLLAR. FOR KNOWING WHICH PIECE OF WIRE TO REPLACE: 29½ DOLLARS."

I broke up.

"And you know what the Prime Minister said to me?"

I shook my head.

"He called me when he got the bill and he said, 'Art, you're absolutely right. You're a man who knows the value of things. *I* only knew the price.'"

Bob Beamon
Memphis, Tennessee

Dear Bob:

That incredible record-breaking jump of yours at the '68 Olympics was the most thrilling athletic feat I've ever witnessed, not just because I love to see a good man do his best, but because you jumped better than your best—better than you were actually "capable" of. *That* kind of miracle happens only once or twice in a lifetime. It happened to me, too. The tragic thing is that there are miracles possible for everyone everyday which *never* happen.

Jesse O.

If one of the biggest things I've learned lately is that most people can't do what *I* think they can, I also hold hard to the gut knowledge that they can do *more* than *they* think they can.

On October 18, 1968, a boy just old enough to vote got ready to take his first broad jump at the Mexico City Olympics. The farthest that boy had ever done before was a little over twenty-seven feet. The farthest anyone else anywhere had ever done was a little over twenty-seven feet. Bob Beamon was the young man.

He jumped an impossible distance that October day.

Actually, Bob didn't jump. He flew.

I'd been down there near the pit, watching the athletes. I think the broad jump has always really been my favorite event. Because at its best, it *is* like flying.

There was a peculiar looseness about Bob before he took his jump. I'd seen it only several other times in my life. Twice I'd felt it myself—before I broke the world's broad jump record at Ann Arbor, and the Olympic mark at Berlin.

When he ran down the runway, he gathered speed with an unusual ease. But nobody—me included—dreamed what was going to happen until he shot up into the air. Even then, we didn't dream anything like twenty-nine feet.

Bob went up high, almost too high. You want an arc so you can stay in the air longer and have your forward thrust carry you farther, but you don't want to waste any thrust on going up instead of out, either.

Beamon didn't. He cut it fine—perfect. Also, he had more thrust than any man who's ever jumped. A *lot* more. When he finally came down, we couldn't believe it.

They measured the jump. Then remeasured it. Twenty-nine feet, two and a half inches.

Maybe that still doesn't mean much to you. Maybe you're an accountant or a housewife or a student not interested or knowledgeable in sports. Well, if you're an accountant, what Bob Beamon did is the same as throwing away the computer and getting it all done in your head faster. If you're a housewife, it's the same as getting it all done by nine thirty in the morning. If you're a student, it's like graduating summa cum laude without ever cracking a book.

I was the first to congratulate him. I wanted more than to shake his hand. I sensed what had just happened there—the true miracle of it—and *that's* what I wanted to grasp.

"What can I tell *you,* Jesse?" he said. "The mental, physical, emotional, who knows what? It all came together, man! You try for years. *You* know. You try and try. Then one day—for one swinging minute—I guess it all just works."

Our whole lives we strive for that one great moment that makes all the sorrow and sickness and suffering worth something. If we're lucky, we achieve one. If we're incredibly fortunate, we have a few.

What does it take? It takes what Bob said, putting it all together—all the parts of yourself. It takes a human miracle.

But miracles happen, baby.

Bob Beamon made it happen, other men and women have made them happen. You might have to strive almost your whole life for just a few seconds of one. But it's worth it. Man, how it's worth it. Because—though it might have a corny ring to some sophisticates—the striving is ennobling. What counts is that day-in, day-out exercise of your character, your guts, your free will, which makes the you that hurts and the you that's joy and the you that's tired and the you that won't quit—the child and man, the sadist and savior—all come together. And what almost everyone seems to miss these days is that we *all* own the one ingredient that ultimately puts it together, the one ingredient that is the *real* miracle: our free will.

It never changes. It's always there. You can't see it, can't touch it. It isn't ever a line in an almanac or a film of a body jumping into the air. It's something inside you, something which helps you to go on before you know it, and never leaves you once you do. As Tommy said in *Brigadoon,* "Sometimes it's what you believe in, not the things you can see or analyze away, that are the most real."

I read last year where Dave Sime, the talented American runner who came in second in the hundred in the 1960 Olympics (and went on to become a doctor), wanted to try a comeback. He was thirty-five years old. Painful? Yes. But I understood. I felt that way more than once. And even past thirty-five. Now and then when I drift off to sleep, time dissolves, 1936 somehow becomes 1956 or even 1972, and I see myself out there, but not *then,* now—*now*—putting it all together somehow for just one more brief slice of time—

That golden moment dies hard. And it *shouldn't* die.

After *Blackthink* came out, Robert Lipsyte asked in *The New York Times* if I really expected my people to make it just through positive thinking and free will. In many ways, he was right. I'd made some mistakes. But in one deeper way, I don't think I'd erred. A letter written not long ago to a Chicago newspaper from a young black man probably tells it better than anything I've been able to say:

> I am a black young adult, age 23, and a Viet Nam war veteran.
>
> We poor blacks can advance in spite of any ghetto. Both of my parents dropped out of grammar school, but I defied the gangs and finished CVS. Now, by having served in Viet Nam, I shall enter Fisk University under the GI Bill of Education this fall.

> Anyone who wishes may read, read, and read at no cost at the library on Kimbark near 63rd Street and improve his grammar as I am still trying to do. Good grades, and especially the GI Bill of Education for men or women vets, will take care of any college expenses. It can be done—I know.

It *can* be done. *Knowing* that it can is the first crucial step in doing it. Free will never changes. It hasn't since we came down out of the trees a million years ago, and it won't be any different when we live on Mars and Jupiter a million years from now. That unchanging free will, *that ability to change,* is the definition of man.

And manhood.

Probably *I* haven't changed enough. But at least I can say, even while writing this, that *I'm still changing.* The Jesse Owens of 1922 sure wasn't the Jesse Owens of 1942 and, though it's just three years since I wrote my first book, if a fifteen- or twenty-year-old can have a couple of years make such a crucial difference in his life, why not a man of almost sixty?

Why *not?*

Okay, you've got two fouls on you. You're scared as hell. Yet as long as a man has that one chance left, he's still in the race.

As you read this, I'll be—or already have been—at the 1972 Olympics in Munich, Germany. For me, it's a kind of going back to my roots. When you're nearly sixty years of age, you seem to get closer to your bittersweet beginnings with each passing day. Of course—even though I've truly come to feel as though *all* people are *my* people—my real beginnings aren't in European soil with stadiums of cheering people. Part of them are rooted in the beauty of Columbus trees. More are rooted in the hunger of Cleveland sidewalks.

But the deepest parts of all are sunk in an Alabama sharecropping shack. Winter is coming—a cruel, always shockingly cold winter, because of the winds, the winds which penetrate all the way through you because the cardboard of the little house can't stop them. Yet now it's September and the sun beats down so hard you wonder to God how your father can stay out there in the white man's fields hour after hour after hour. The white-hot sun takes your own breath away, even though you're hidden under the overhang of the makeshift shack, forcing the crackling ground under your bare feet to split. The first breeze of afternoon, hinting ever so slightly of cruel January, sweeps the dry dust up into your mouth and nostrils and you cough, cough till it seems you'll never stop, cough not only in your throat but through your lungs all the way down to your gut. Then it's later, dark, you're in "bed"—a potato sack on the floor in one corner of the big room. You're coughing again. Coughing blood. Your mother is whispering to your father, pain on her face. "What'll we do, Henry? The boy's going to die *this* winter sure. What'll we *do?*" But is it that Alabama shack? Or a hospital room in Miami? An oxygen tent over me. Everything hazy. Ruth there, pain on her face. Whispering to the doctor. "Do something—please *do* something. His lungs can't take one more of these double pneumonias!" The doctor's lips moving mutely. But I know what he's saying. What the doctor in Chicago said. "It's all up to him now, Mrs. Owens. It all comes down to his will to live. . . ." Breathing harder. Lungs aching. Chest burning. Choking, can't get enough air. Because of the pneumonia, or because I'm out there again, running? Doesn't matter. The hurt feels so fine, *wherever* you are. For the struggle is what it's all about.

As long as you're locked in, you know that somewhere there's an outside.

Dear Ruth,

If ever a wife—

Love,

J.

I began this book with a painful story of how a black shoeshine man who hardly knew me felt I was a bigot because of moving to Phoenix from the south side of Chicago. Maybe I ought to end it by telling you exactly why I moved to Phoenix.

I went to Phoenix to live first of all because Ruth wanted me to. She wanted me to because she felt it would save my life.

Cliché or no cliché, my wife has never been sick a day. Our old Dr. Rogers in Chicago, who passed away a few years ago, used to say, "Ruth—the good Lord made you healthy so that Jesse would be kept alive."

In September of 1971, I didn't work the entire month. It was virtually the first time in fifty years I'd gone more than three days without flying or speaking somewhere. I did it because my doctor told me that if I didn't take off all of September, I wouldn't be here in October.

It had begun in August. The usual chest cold that I couldn't shake. I tried to get rid of it in Boston, in L.A., an afternoon in Chicago, a busy weekend in New York, but no way. When I got to Tampa, *it* shook *me*.

My doctor had already diagnosed it long distance as pneumonia, but I told him I simply couldn't come back. He'd called the drugstore in the hotel where I was and put me on a strong antibiotic. "That's a vicious cough—much as we needed it, you shouldn't have come down here," they told me when I finally got to Tampa. But I figured if I could just make it to the warm South, I'd be all right.

The pneumonia had started six years before, during the tax thing. The last time my doctor had warned me that things were different from 1965. At nearly sixty, a lot of the leg muscles and energy might still be left from the original "world's fastest human," but the lung tissue wasn't.

I spent those thirty September days in our Michigan summer home (the best investment, by the way—hell, the *only* one—I've ever made).

It wasn't easy, even though walking from room to room made me gasp. I *love* to move, you see. Beneath everything else *that's* what I *am*. No matter how much I learn to stop and smell the flowers, most of me will always be the guy leaving on the next plane.

But Phoenix has made a difference. It probably did save my life. I'll never miss those Chicago winters, for one thing. And for another, in Chicago I couldn't walk out of my front door without two dozen people catching me before I got to the plane and asking me to do this or that. I've just never known how to say *no*. So the best thing for me was not to be asked as much.

Chicago was high-rise living, too, and that always bugged me in a special way. Before the tax thing, we had a ten-room apartment, all spread out like a half-mile track. Even with the three girls living there, I had a feeling of space. I could breathe. I almost could run the 220 there!

But the high-rise was something else. I never really felt anything but cramped in it, didn't even like to sleep in it, let alone stay a whole day there the few times that was possible. And walking out of it, what did you see?

Phoenix is different; it's still country. We have a house. There's golf the year 'round. Less people on my back. And, yes, less racial tension.

A selfish cop-out? I don't think so. I'll be working thousands of hours every year to improve things. But if there was any truth in what the old shoeshine man said, I'll have to accept it. Because Phoenix is more than less this or less that. Phoenix is Ruth.

Talk about long-distance races. Though she doesn't like to admit it (because we were married for the world to see a couple of years later), Ruth and I first secretly became man and wife forty-three years ago. We'd fallen in love long before even that, having met in grammar school in Cleveland. Her folks had come up from the South, Georgia, trying to escape the poverty and degradation down there just as mine had.

It wasn't easy getting married at sixteen even in those days. My best buddy, Dave Albritton, had to come along and bring *his* girl friend so we'd have witnesses. And we couldn't tie the knot in Cleveland or even the whole State of Ohio. We finally found a willing Justice of the Peace in Erie, Pennsylvania!

We got there in a broken down 1914 Model T that Dave and I had scraped like mad to down-pay four dollars for. Our wedding dinner was a hotdog with all the relish you could wedge between it and the bun. Our champagne was two soft drinks. There wasn't a honeymoon. We hurried back to Cleveland so that no one would suspect anything, living for the better part of a year with Ruth at her house and me at mine.

Finally, I couldn't take it any longer. We broke the news to our shocked parents and took a one-room apartment of our own. Ruth got full-time work in Wagner's Beauty Shop and I kept my usual assortment of jobs so we could make ends meet in our seven-dollar-a-month Home Sweet Home. And it was. Maybe the sweetest. I know it was for Ruth in some ways.

Well, if there are things living within me that haven't changed, the most cherished is Ruth Solomon. She never complained when I moved her from city to city, state to state, forced her to make new homes—and she made them *real* homes—in each place, raising our girls, picking *me* up whenever I stumbled in my sometimes lonely race. Even though she's a very private person—sometimes I envy her a little—Ruth always found time to do as much charitable work in her life as I have. Not as chairman with her name on the letterhead (which she easily could have been as "Mrs. Jesse Owens"), but simply as an anonymous hard worker who consistently dug in and helped human beings when they needed help. Most often, they were ghetto human beings. Yet when the more violent waves of ghetto extremism started sweeping Chicago's south side a few years ago, they weren't able to sweep aside the common sense and quiet dignity inside of Ruth.

I remember a party we went to at the home of one of our daughters. A young extremist in his twenties strolled up to her and, instead of politely saying hello, crudely offered the black handshake that was "in" that month.

Ruth didn't move a muscle. "I don't know anything about *that*," she said softly to him.

Ruth's old-fashionedness hasn't stopped her from staying youthful and progressive, though. It's just that to her you can tell most about someone not so much by what they say as how they say it.

Like the time we spent an evening with a white couple we didn't know too well. The man was the new head of one of the biggest, best-backed inner-city organizations in the Midwest. He wanted my help. At first I was more than glad to give it to him.

As the night wore on, though, I felt uneasy. You couldn't talk about the weather without his telling you how he was going to change it for the better. And yet, whenever he'd talk about anything—which was almost 90 percent of the time—it wasn't enthusiasm or even energy that came through. I heard hostility.

When it got to be ten thirty, I figured the only way to end the evening on a pleasant note was with a little music. He'd said he loved music. We went into my den and I put some jazz on the stereo.

"Jazz—that's plastic, Jesse," he criticized when a Ramsey Lewis record dropped down. "Don't you have any rock? Or soul. *You* should have *soul* music, Jesse." I'd had a jazz-soul-pop radio show for years—started it before this guy started shaving. I didn't make much money from the show, did it mainly because I love music and needed the break—even when I had to tape it a month in advance because of travel commitments.

I told him to take a look at my record collection and pick whatever he liked. He found a couple. I offered to put them on. He refused, wanted to do it himself. He had to control everything.

Only he didn't control it too well. The turmoil inside him even came through when he dropped the needle down hard before the band that he wanted on each record. He couldn't just let the whole record play, hear them all the way through. He had to play his favorite choices for you right then, this band on this record, that band on that one, then turn them over and do the same. Each time, he jerked the arm into place until the records were ruined. I knew I'd probably need a new needle, too. But what really disturbed me was that this fellow was going to control a lot more than my stereo, and for a lot longer than one night.

I'd politely let it be known that I had to catch a plane at 8:45 the next morning, but the rock and "soul" lover didn't get the message. He wasn't a good listener. Eleven became midnight and then one A.M. My hints grew more obvious, but he was too "involved" with talking about all the things he was going to change. Finally, I couldn't take it. "Look," I told him, "sometimes *I'm* so concerned just getting my *own* self together that I don't feel up to changing the whole damn world!"

He answered me almost before I was through saying it. "Sure, sure," he shot back, missing the point. "You've got to save your own soul before you can save anyone else's. Goes without saying. But I've done it, Jesse. I'm there. Know what's plastic and what isn't." It was about the hundredth time he'd used the word *plastic*.

They finally left at twenty to three. I gratefully, wearily and not a little angrily watched them walk down the hall in their barefoot sandals, jeans and peace medallions. As soon as I'd shut the door, Ruth turned to me.

"God in heaven, Jesse," she whispered. "The man can't even play a phonograph record without scratching it. And he expects to heal people's souls!"

In a way, it's ironic that we left Chicago after almost twenty years, because people like that, incidents like that, happened so much more in Chicago than in Detroit or Cleveland or Columbus. Not that we don't miss the girls, their husbands, our grandchildren, but we kept the home in Michigan and will spend every summer we have left with them up there. All in all, I think we'll have more time with our family and get to know each other better.

I'm honestly not knocking Chicago. Things happened there because the city was the melting pot of America. That's where the action was. Yet Chicago *was* the one place in our lives that scared Ruth. No matter what kind of hard times we'd had before moving there, she'd been able to meet the obstacles without a single word. But a few months after we settled in Chicago, for the first time I could see that she wasn't herself.

"What's the matter, baby?" I asked. She tried to tell me it was nothing, but when I pressed Ruth finally let it out.

"This isn't like the other places we've lived, Jesse. People try and hurt you here." It was true, though I'd been too busy to really think about it. Chicago just wasn't "home." Most people either wanted to use you or put you down.

At the time, I was working with the Harlem Globetrotters in an executive capacity. The Trotters, of course, were the first all-black basketball team to make it in the white world and, in those days, they were the best team around. They were run by a five-foot tall middle-aged Jewish man, Abe Saperstein. I told him about the bad feeling Ruth and I and the girls had encountered and Abe started coming over to the house and inviting Ruth and the girls to his own with some *real* friends, black *and* white. It was Abe who finally made Ruth feel the girls would be all right in Chicago.

And they were.

But in almost twenty years, *we* never quite got used to it. Maybe some of it was the impersonalness of a metropolis. Chicago was a lot bigger somehow than the closely knit World War II Detroit or the Cleveland of the twenties. I've traveled the world a hundred times, but maybe I'm mostly a small-town boy at heart with the dirt—good and bad—of the Alabama cottonfields still under my manicured nails. Ruth, too. Even when I was making close to $100,000 a year, she hung her own wallpaper, painted the unpapered rooms herself.

Phoenix is more like the old days, with the fresh quality of the West added. Because of that, I'm spending less time in New York and Chicago, South America and Africa, spending a little less time too, I'll admit, with crime problems and race problems, with people who want to start civic projects or want to present some award to someone. But those hours are being spent better. And the ones I'm saving are making up for lost time with the most worthwhile human being I've ever known.

And that's no plastic establishment nostalgia.

I don't know, though, if I can ever learn one final lesson from Ruth, if I can gain that remarkable quality from her which lets her progress while never changing her fundamentals, lets her grow older gracefully while staying young inside. Almost sixty or not, Phoenix or not, I still know I'll drop in my tracks someday. And I won't really mind if it comes sooner than it should, as long as I'm making tracks when I drop.

That's about the only thing we argue about.

She'll say something or not want to do something we

used to do when we were young. "You're getting old!" I'll snap.

"We're *both* getting old, Jesse," she'll answer quietly. "The only difference between us is that *you* won't recognize it."

She's right. But knowing it hasn't helped me to change that last thing about myself which probably should be changed. I *can't.* I *won't,* I guess. Each day, in some way or other, I've just got to stay the world's fastest human. Because of it, I'll never have her peace inside myself.

But maybe that's what setting records is all about.

I won't tell you it doesn't scare me sometimes. But the fear passes with the next flight or golf game or even the next brisk walk to the drugstore to buy a paper.

How can a man like me ever prepare for being old?

A P.S.

I don't believe in loving my neighbor.

No matter how often everyone today shouts that *that* will be the only solution to our problems, I don't see it. You can't love someone just because he lives next to you or is a part of your community. Or a part of the human community. You're lucky if you can love —really love—your wife, your kids, a handful, just a handful, of other people in your entire lifetime.

When the upper middle-class white couple cruelly discusses the race problem at dinner with their friends while totally ignoring the colored maid who serves their food, *love* isn't needed. When a long-haired— though I hope it's clean-haired—hippie or Afro-haired job applicant sits in the personnel manager's office trying to make a living peaceably, *love* isn't the issue. When the police tap the phone of a Martin Luther King or, conversely, when a white high school coach brings breakfast to a skinny black kid fresh off an Alabama tenant farm, love or lack of it aren't the solution or the psychology.

Many of the southern plantation owners actually did love their slaves at times, you know. And what of those "flower children" today who say they feel love toward everyone and then rip off someone else's property— or even human lives in the case of the Manson "family"? It doesn't take a genius to figure out that people who need to love everybody are usually trying to make up for never having been loved by anybody.

Maybe if everyone weren't so hung up on loving everyone else, the world could finally start to get it together. I've been around quite awhile now, and honestly don't think there are a handful of men on this earth who've known more people than I have. I've seen real love, and hate—and the overwhelmingly common in-betweens. And one thing I know: Love isn't something you can carry around with you and distribute like Girl Scout cookies. But there *is* something just as important that you *can* take with you wherever you go, something you can control because, sweet as love is, it can't be controlled. You either feel it or you don't. But this other "something" you can give—and get—merely by virtue of your being a human being. Unless you stop being a *human* being. One little Abidjanian boy in particular will always remind me best of that.

I never knew his name, but I certainly did get to know *him*. He came up to me the third day I was there, after some of the ballyhoo had subsided, and tried to ask me a question. I don't know much French, Ivory Coast's national language, and he just was a bare beginner at English, so communication was pretty rough. Try as we did, we couldn't get through to one another.

The next day I was walking near the huts with the Prime Minister when the boy breathlessly appeared.

"Jesse Owens—want ask Jesse Owens!"

Prime Minister Houphouët-Boigny nodded to the youngster, smiling a little. "*Yes?*"

"Jesse Owens," he began again in a thick accent. "How—how you—how Jesse Owens—" He stopped in frustration, pointed down at my shoes. Then he began one more time. "Jesse Owens—how Jesse Owens—with —how you with—"

He just couldn't make it. I tried to help but, suddenly, tears in his eyes, he turned and bolted. I started after him, but the boy could really run and in a moment I'd lost him in a nearby field.

I didn't forget him, though, found myself looking around for him more than once in the following days as I walked and worked and played and talked amidst group after group of youngsters. But the days were so full and raced by so quickly that before I knew it the last morning had come and I was packing.

As I left the Prime Minister's home for the limousine that would drive me to the waiting plane, I took a last look at the beautiful countryside. There was a good feeling within me. I'd learned in Ivory Coast—learning I could take back and use, possibly help our government to use. Too, I frankly felt I'd done a good job there. Not only the job Secretary of State Rogers had sent me for, but a job no one can ever tell you to do, something more intangible than State Department P.R. releases or even the tractors we send. Of course, a lot of people could've done what I helped to do in Ivory Coast. But it happened that I was the one lucky enough to be given the opportunity, and it made me feel right inside. Only one piece of "unfinished business" stuck in my mind. That young boy. What had he wanted to say to me? How important might the answer have been?

In the car were two other visiting dignitaries. The driver, an Abidjanian orphan of about eighteen who had been raised in the huts, turned the key and the motor roared. Just as the limousine was pulling away,

I heard an insistent knock at my window. Running alongside the car was the boy!

"Stop! Please!" I shouted to the driver. He did and I rolled down the window. "Hi, there!" I greeted. I was so happy to see him. I'd missed working things out with the little tyke more than I'd known.

"Jesse Owens," he said proudly. "I want ask you. Okay?"

I almost laughed. What he must have gone through to learn just those words alone during the last week! "Okay," I answered.

"How could—how could Jesse Owens—run so fast —with—with—small foots?"

I did laugh. But I nodded too. It's true—I only wear an eight shoe, have almost tiny feet for a man of my build. People used to talk about it a lot when I was actively competing. But no one had mentioned it now for thirty years.

"That made it easier, *better*," I told him slowly, watching his face to see if he understood.

He wrinkled up his unlined little face. "Why make it . . . easier-better?"

"Because I didn't have as much—" I gestured, lifting my hands in the air as if they were holding something heavy "—to lift up. Or—to put down," I said, making the opposite gesture.

For a second he frowned. Then, suddenly, understanding flooded his face.

"Yes!" he almost shrieked. "Little foot! Not so much lift up put down!" He began nodding wildly.

Then all at once he stopped.

He reached out his hand to mine.

"Thank you, Jesse Owens," he said as we shook, though it sounded more like "Ankoo, Jizzee Ooons."

"Call me just . . . Jesse," I told him.

"Ankoo . . . *Jizzee,*" he said.

We broke our handshake, waved, and the auto pulled away once more. I watched him from the rear window till he was just a speck on the horizon. It was then I noticed that someone else was speaking to me. One of the dignitaries from another country was grumbling about the delay.

I probed deep into the man's eyes with my own. "That's what we came here for, isn't it?"

He looked down. There was silence inside the car for a couple of minutes. I felt ashamed that I'd lost my temper, told him so. "You certainly *love* these youngsters, don't you?" he replied.

I put my hand on his arm. "No," I told him. "I can't really say that I *love* them. Love is such a *rare* feeling."

"But what then?" he inquired. "Look how they feel toward *you.*"

I nodded. "I'm grateful for that," I said. "But it isn't because I give them love. If they do feel strongly toward me, it's because I give them *respect.*"

"What?" he said, as the car turned a final corner and the plane that would take us away from Ivory Coast came into sight.

"*Respect,*" I answered him. "Just *respect.*"

Whatever I failed to give to so many youngsters through the years, to my family, to myself, because of changes I made too late or ones I may never make, whatever black parts of me—and I mean parts *beneath* the skin—had made Jesse Owens *less* human, one thing I've learned is that every human being deserves respect simply because he is a human being. And being different—or bad sometimes—doesn't lose you the franchise. We've all got some Hitler in us. If anything can drive that out, change us for the better, it starts with respect.

One young Ivory Coast boy gave it to me, and I know I'm a more human being for it. Just as I hope he's a little better for the respect I tried to show in return.

Though maybe I do love him a little, too.